Dream Walking

By Donna Rose-Heim

COVER PHOTO BY RACHAEL NEEDHAM GREEN

First published by Dog Ear Publishing
4010 W. 86th Street, Ste H
Indianapolis, IN 46268
www.dogearpublishing.net

ISBN: 978-159858-377-9

This book is printed on acid-free paper.

Printed in the United States of America

TABLE OF CONTENTS

Introduction

Remember for a moment some of the things you dreamed about as a child. Perhaps you imagined boxes turning into spaceships or rags becoming royal robes. Maybe you dreamed of traveling to far away lands or inventing products that would save people's lives. Did you have children you named and cherished? How did you dream and imagine your future?

What do you dream about now? What images and feelings fill your mind? Do you allow yourself to really nurture and step into your dreams and the dreams God desires to share with you?

In my own life, I found that the busyness of being a mom, a minister, a wife and a friend somehow drained my desire to dream. As I focused more and more on getting things done, my mind became focused on the material world and events that happened to me, to my family or to my church. I was incredibly responsible, however my creativity and joy came only in spurts. Despair was a shadow that followed me, sometimes consuming me, sometimes at a distance. There were interludes where I stepped into life with a full heart – at retreats I led or attended, inspired moments with my children, worship that raised my heart to feel God anew, or wonderful moments with my husband – yet, something was missing.

I was shaken one day when one of my sons said, "Mom, why are you so angry all the time?" Granted, he was in trouble at the moment, but his words carried more truth than I wanted to see. I began to observe myself and other women. I realized the same thing was happening to far too many of us. I kept hearing conversations between women that drifted readily to negative, weary or angry thinking. I watched the faces of women whose lips were permanently formed into a frown. Women, of all types, were dragging themselves from thing to thing without a strong sense of being called by God to be a significant part of some overarching purpose. I began to seek and pray. I read books, went to seminars and kept seeking some thread that would guide me.

It was in the midst of my seeking that my dreaming became more active. Both at night and in the day, I began to dream dreams again. The dreaming I had so naturally done as a child started to renew itself. I struggled to understand dreaming and to make it a vital part of my daily life, rather than a side step at a retreat. How could I reclaim the God-given ability to dream in the midst of my busy life? As I pursued these questions, my passion and desire to dream grew.

What is dreaming really? Psychologists suggest that our dreams are the arena in which our minds have unfettered opportunities to work through our most pressing challenges. But I began to believe dreams are far more than this. What if God gave us the gift of dreaming to sometimes create an unfiltered path to God's desires for us? What if our dreaming could happen not only when we are asleep, but also when we are awake? I thought of Jacob, Joseph, Peter, Paul, Mother Teresa and Dr. Martin Luther King, Jr. who had their lives transformed because of their willingness to pursue the truths God showed to them in dreams or visions. What if God still desires to transform our thinking and actions through our dreams? What if in our rational world we have shut down this form of communication? What if by dreaming with God, we could literally change the world by first changing ourselves as we see a part of what God dreams and desires?

Throughout the scriptures and human history, it is dreaming and imagining that begin change and opportunity. Think of the woman in Mark 5:25-34 who had been bleeding for twelve long years. She had spent everything she owned on every medical treatment she could find. The cures had left her penniless and growing increasingly weak. Her bleeding had made her unclean (Leviticus 15:19-33) and had cut her off from much of life. Had her family deserted her? Where did she live? We know none of this. We do know that she never totally gave up on dreaming she could be well. She kept seeking and hoping and believing. When she heard Jesus was coming to her area, she knew he was her answer. It wouldn't take much, just one touch. She snuck into the crowd, hoping no one would notice her. It was so hard to work her way closer to him. She couldn't quite reach Jesus. She stretched her hand out just one more time and managed to barely touch one of the tassels on his robe. Immediately she felt a power radiate through her body and she was healed! The hemorrhaging stopped! It was a miracle!

Then it happened. Jesus turned and asked, "Who touched my garments?" The woman was terribly afraid and exhilarated all at the same time. She had not asked Jesus' permission to touch him. Would he be angry? Would he remove this amazing healing? Would he…? Then she saw his eyes. They looked gently at her as she fell down before him and told him everything, everything, just as it had happened. She spared nothing from him. It was as though the crowd had completely disappeared and Jesus and she were alone. He lifted her to her feet and said, "Daughter, your faith has made you well; go in peace, and be healed of your disease." (Mark 5:34 NRSV)

I can only imagine this woman's joy as she turned to begin her life anew. Not only had she been made well, she had been made whole! Jesus had claimed her as a daughter in God's family. The whole world was open to her again. Her willingness to step into her dream for healing had given her far more than she had hoped.

It all started with a dream. A little piece of God's spirit encouraging this unnamed woman to step out in faith and believe! Before she had only seen the walls of her illness. Now she could see first a window and then a door to hope with God's help. Before Jesus there was isolation and fear. Now she could see herself as a daughter of God. What if she had not dared to dream? What a loss it would have been for her, for the crowd and for those of us who are inspired generations later by her faith and courage.

God has given us so many gifts to help us know God and God's ways. Creation, the gift of Jesus, the Holy Spirit, scripture and personal experiences with God, all guide us to know Who God is and how God desires us to experience God. Dreams and dreaming are one way we can engage with God and continue to grow in our understanding of God's desires for the world and for us. Some of our dreams specifically challenge us to move forward in our faith, while others are more of an exercise field to work out unfinished events and hopes. When we, like the woman who was healed, open ourselves to dream with God, we are given the encouragement we need to step out in new ways. Rather than allowing things to be as they are, God through the Holy Spirit, moves us to believe things could be different. Like Jesus, we begin to see five loaves and two fish can become a feast, a net that is empty can be made full of fish, or a woman who had many husbands can be worthy of saving. Our dreams can become a door for God to help us venture into God's ideas and creativity.

What about you? Are you willing to venture into the dreams God has for you? Are you desiring greater wellness and wholeness? Are you someone who is seeking to make a difference in your own life and contribute to the lives of others? If so, then I invite you to rekindle your God-given gift of dreaming as you enter into 28 days of dream walking with God. You will practice and build your ability to dream and listen for God as you engage with scripture, pray, explore and most importantly give yourself an opportunity to dream with God.

Whether you are intentionally dream walking already with God, or if this is a new idea for you, the study is designed to help you accept and glean more from your dreams with God. Through your dreaming, you may just reawaken dream walking in those you touch. Who knows what God could do with thousands of women committed to dreaming and intentionally pursuing their God-given dreams?

Men are certainly welcome to read this book, however I have intentionally written it with women in my mind and heart. In my own life, and in ministering with women, I have been astounded at what can and does happen when women dare to dream and act on those dreams. I have also wept at the loss God must feel as women, created in God's image, have all but given up on dreaming and seeking because of their hurt, pain or weariness. God wants more for us and from us. My prayer for every reader is to find what her heart has been seeking to grow more deeply into the calling of being a daughter of God, with all the privileges and responsibilities this brings.

To gain the most from this book, I strongly encourage you to set aside a daily prayer time of 15-30 minutes. Should you miss a day, dust yourself off and pick up where you left off. Part of the gift I hope this book brings to you is to experience the value of a daily discipline of time alone with God practicing dream walking. I encourage you to give yourself the gift of this time each day if you are not already doing so. You may also enjoy exploring the study with a partner or group of women for the four-week period.

Each day has a focus verse, a longer passage for those who like additional reading, a dream or message to ponder and then questions to engage the reader in interpreting the message. Specific opportunities to live out the interpretations you have experienced with God are suggested. Each week has a different physical act to help integrate the learnings. It is a reminder to live out the interpretations in thought, feelings and actions throughout the day. These can easily be repeated or shared with those with whom you are in community. By repeating each activity for seven days, my hope is that it will become familiar enough for you to use spontaneously in the future.

Following each day, is a Daily Prayer Journal. Each part of the journal is there to guide you through a process of opening, receiving and responding to God. I encourage you to use it daily as a companion to this book and as a guide for your future dream walking. Please feel free to duplicate this form and use it for yourself and others.

I give thanks to God for the gifts of my parents, Ruth and Kenneth Heim, my siblings, Valerie, Kenna and Ralph, my husband, Bill, and our children, Nate, Zach, Elizabeth, Christina and Dan. They have taught me many of the nuances of dream walking as they and I have grown in love. I appreciate their willingness to encourage me to dream and seek together greater richness in life. I also want to thank my friend, Kathy Little, for her unending encouragement and inspiration. It is these loved ones, along with too many others to name, that have caused me to write this book and continue to lead retreats to encourage women to dream walk with God.

Rejoicing at the Bottom of Crater Lake in Oregon
By Kim Shuman

Day 1

"How weighty to me are your thoughts, O God! How vast is the sum of them! I try to count them—they are more than the sand; I come to the end—I am still with you." Psalm 139:17 & 18   NRSV

Reading for the Day: Psalm 139:1-18

Dreaming: God, You Did Good Today!

When our son, Zach, was 2 years old, it seemed that I was perpetually running behind. Motherhood had somehow changed my practice of being on time. On one beautiful spring morning, I was due at a church meeting at precisely 9 a.m. It was fifteen minutes before 9 and I knew if everything went just right I could get Zach to his school and me to the church with one minute to spare. The last shoe was found and tied and we finally made it out the door. With my eyes on the goal of the car, Zach suddenly stopped dead in front of me on the sidewalk. I almost flipped over him and was starting to say all three of his names in my most motherly voice, when Zach raised up his small arms to the heavens. With a voice that will forever radiate in my ears, and most likely in God's as well, he proclaimed, "God, you did SO good today!"

I looked up at the sky and the trees and then into the eyes of my son. How right Zach was, "God you did do SO good today!" We stopped and looked together at all the beauty. Each piece of creation came from one of God's dreams. The breeze that kissed our cheeks, the sounds of birds singing, the admiration of God's creativity in my son's eyes, all were gifts to us. My son did not know the greatest beauty I saw that day. I realized that Zach's thoughts were on his Creator, while mine were busy with details. Yes, I was certainly late to my meeting. However, I made the most important appointment that day. When I arrived ten minutes late, I shared the story of Zach's keen awareness of God and of the astounding gifts God placed lovingly in creation. Even those a bit frustrated with my lateness began to focus on what God was doing around us. Our meeting was blessed with laughter and inspiration. We accomplished a great deal of planning in a relatively short time – most likely more than if I had arrived on time and rushing to beat the clock.

Zach taught me a lesson that day which becomes more important to me as I seek to live my life actively pursuing the dreams of God. If I want to step into the dreams of God, I must prepare my heart and mind to notice and receive God. I cannot afford to allow my mind to focus haphazardly on things of passing significance that may diminish my receptivity. As I choose to fill my mind with an appreciation of God's thoughts and gifts, I am slowly transformed. It is as though the more I dwell on our awesome God, the wider the gates to God's dreams and presence become for me. Amazingly, when I focus on God's abundant love and care, those around me are also touched. The passion for God's presence multiplies and people begin to open their hearts and minds to hear God's dreams, almost like a symphony of dreaming.

From the beginning of time God has been a dreamer of great dreams. Who could have imagined the earth and all of its beauty being formed from chaos? Who could possibly have dreamed up the design of a human body with such an intricate system of cells and organs? Who else could continue to dream that we would be partners with God, even when so many times each of us has failed? God continues to dream and continues to choose to give us the gift of dreaming. Are we ready for it?

The first part of dream walking is essential. You must make your heart and your mind ready to receive God and God's dreams. It means many times a day opening yourself to recognize God's presence - just like Zach – even when you may not feel like it. This becomes an ongoing process, one which will become more natural for you as you practice it daily. I encourage you to choose over and over again to focus on that which is excellent, lovely and holy. (Philippians 4:4-9) When your mind begins to drift to thoughts of chaos, fear, anger, weariness or lack, replace these with clear thoughts of

God and God's dreams. Make your imagery clear, positive and strong. By doing so, you make ready a place within you for God's dreams to dwell and multiply.

Some of the truths about God and images that I ponder include:

God loves all people and wants to be in relationship with us. I picture God calling people of all colors, shapes and sizes to come and join God in a circle. In John 3:16, the gift of Jesus, God's son, is clearly given to "the world," not just for some part of the world. Jesus demonstrated this truth as he spoke to the wealthy and to the poor, to the Jew and to the Samaritan, to women and to men, etc.

God smiles when we work together to bring love, hope and possibilities to the world. I see people building a home with someone in need and God smiling. Jesus took the question, "Teacher, what shall I do to inherit eternal life?" and turned it into a lesson on loving God and one's neighbor. Read this story in Luke 10:25-37.

There are more than enough resources of money, time and talents for all of us to be partners with God in miracles. The image of Jesus feeding 5000 people with the help of a child comes to mind for me. In Luke 10, Jesus sends out 70 people to preach the gospel, heal the sick and proclaim, "The kingdom of God has come near to you." Luke 10:9 RSV Spreading the gospel was not something Jesus desired to do alone.

God's ways are love, accountability, partnership, forgiveness and grace. I see God rejoicing when I take real steps to pursue one of God's dreams. See the story of the Prodigal Son in Luke 15:11-32.

I choose to dream and ponder things like these as I open myself more fully to God and God's dreams. What do you choose to dream and ponder about God?

Interpreting the Dream

What are some of God's creations you love to ponder?

What are some of the truths about God you desire to bring fully into your mind, heart and life? Write these below.

Repeat these numerous times each day, particularly if you find your mind wandering to thoughts of scarcity or worry. Pick one and focus on it repeatedly throughout the day or repeat the list several times until you have them memorized. If you notice your mind drifting to thoughts that stifle your dreaming, prepare your mind anew with these thoughts of God.

Do you have a recurring dream or thought that God has placed in your heart? If so, describe it here. What is the setting for the dream? Who is in the dream? What sounds, smells and sights are in the dream? How do you feel during and after the dream?

Where and how is it easiest for you to dream with God?

Dream Walking

Sit outside or near a window and breathe deeply in through your nose and out through your mouth three times. Dream for a moment about God's desires. What might they be for the world, for you and for those you will meet? Give thanks for all that you experience in the next 5 – 10 minutes. Be open to all kinds of possibilities. Choose not to think about how these can be accomplished. Honor these dreams by enjoying and savoring them. This is a simple and effective "attitude adjustment" you can use throughout the day to keep your heart and mind fresh and ready for God's indwelling.

Integrating the Dream

Stand tall with your shoulders back. Put your palms together in front of your chest in the praying hands position. Raise them straight up and then open your hands and arms into a large circle. As you do this, think of yourself opening up to God who is within you. You may even want to add with zeal, "God you did SO good today!"

This activity will be repeated for the next seven days to create a familiarity with the experience. Feel free to expand and move in ways that are helpful to your dreaming experience.

Daily Prayer Journal

Date _____   Scripture _____

I rejoice in: (Make these very specific joys and change them every day. They may be savoring a bowl of soup, a healing in a friend, a new job opportunity, etc. The main thing is to be aware of that which gives you and God joy today.)

      1.

      2.

      3.

      4.

      5.

I hear God saying to me in the scripture: (What do you hear in the scripture? How do you respond? What/who do you think about when you read this? What questions does it raise?)

Faith and visualization statements about myself I am creating with God: (These are statements you believe God is creating within you as you dream together. Such as, "I am a creative, abundant, inspirational woman." Or, "I am growing in faith and trust." Eventually this will become a consistent statement until the visualization is realized. For now, write what comes to mind and build on this. You will know when you have found your focus.)

God and I dream about: (Allow yourself to close your eyes and listen. What comes to mind? Be specific. It could be an excellent evaluation, a reconciliation with someone, a cure for AIDS, peace in the Middle East, etc. Do not question the dreams. Just write them down. Periodically review these and see what God and you are doing to fulfill these dreams.)

I commit to do the following things with God today: (These should be very specific and measurable. For example, "I will hug each of my loved ones today and tell them 2 things I love about them (including myself)" instead of, "I will be more loving today." At the beginning of each day's prayer time, review the previous day's list and check off those you have accomplished. Are there any you desire to move into the next day or are they no longer a part of your commitment to God?)

Day 2

"When she could hide him no longer she got a papyrus basket for him, and plastered it with bitumen and pitch; she put the child in it and placed it among the reeds on the bank of the river. His sister stood at a distance, to see what would happen to him." Exodus 2:3 & 4 NRSV

Reading for the Day: Exodus 2:1-10

Dreaming: Dreaming New Realities

The world can be full of things that scare us. Some are very real, while others are creations of our mind. Jochebed, the mother of Moses, lived in a world full of real physical danger. She had seen first hand the cruel killings of Hebrew baby boys. When she gave birth to Moses, she could not imagine herself willingly offering up her son to the hands of murderers. So Jochabed did the best she knew how to do – she hid her baby boy. How hard it must have been to keep the little one quiet. Did she sing to him, hide him in chests or under tables? How did she keep from sharing her pride and joy with others around her? Surely her friends knew she had been pregnant. Did she tell them her baby had died?

In three month's time, Moses was growing and beginning to explore as babies do. It would not be long before he would crawl and then walk. His mother knew she could not hide him much longer. His cries grew louder and more persistent. Perhaps his sister covered his cries with wails of her own. Jochebed must have lifted her voice in pleas for help to the God of Abraham, Sarah and Jacob. Day and night, she must have considered how to save her small son until the day came she dared to dream Moses could have a long and full life.

We are uncertain how the risky answer came to her. Perhaps it was in a dream or a prayer. Or maybe she was just washing clothes, when she realized Pharaoh's daughter often bathed at a certain place each day. How long had she considered building the tiny basket/ship her son would rest in that day? How long did she watch Pharaoh's daughter to see if perhaps she had a spark of kindness and goodness in her eyes – at least enough that she would choose to save a tiny baby? Would she, could she, save this little one's life?

To come out of hiding meant risking Moses' life and possibly hers as well. Yet the cost of hiding became so high that Jochebed was willing to risk failure rather than wait for certain doom to fall. Her step of faith literally gave life to Moses. How amazing that she even received the gift of being his hired nurse maid! And greater still, it was through Moses that all the Hebrews would one day be saved from slavery. What if Moses' mother had been too afraid to dream and try? What if she had hidden and pretended that "everything would be all right?" What if she had failed to see the high cost of her failing to dream and step out in new ways of faith?

Like Jochebed, Pharaoh's daughter is an amazing woman. She stepped out of her role of being subservient to her father's commands to save the child. How did she manage to convince her father the baby was worthy of saving? How did she get him to raise the little boy like a son? Surely people must have talked in the palace and around the city. Yet, somehow, God spoke in her heart. Pharaoh's daughter dared to dream she could become an advocate for this little one. What if she had never believed she could shelter this tiny baby?

As a woman, do you sometimes focus on what is and stop dreaming about what could be with God's help? Day by day, parts of your joy and creativity fade because you allow them to do so from lack of use. You focus on your job to finish just one more special project. You work at being beautiful for your mate and maybe even work for hours to cook a delicious home cooked meal. The children need clothes or have games to attend. You want your friends to know they can depend on you in any situation. And, ah yes, the church, the Chamber of Commerce, your sorority, the Rotary Club, the P.T.A. etc., all have your name down because you are "one of those you ask because she's busy and will get the job done right." You hide behind your fears of stepping out in a different way and look incredibly responsible, yet what do you miss?

What will it take for you to risk living fully into your joy? What will it take for you to open yourself to dream anew of what might be for you and those you love, along with all the thousands you and they may touch? What do you need to dare to dream and to step out in faith in a new direction?

This does not mean the children are not fed or that you necessarily quit your job or friendships and marriage or leave the church, clubs or the P.T.A. It does mean you consciously choose a direction, a direction in which God guides you each day. You willingly come out of an often scripted life and claim your God-given destiny. Dream walking does not look like rising up, doing chores, going to work, watching TV and going to bed again. It means going to your heart where the joy of God dwells in power and light and seeking the dream that will propel you into living out miraculous possibilities. It's taking the time to make a call or a visit when you have the urging. It's writing a book when you are led. It's creating music or dancing or giving a healing touch. It's … You will never know unless you step out in faith, giving yourself time each day to dream and step out of hiding from the "to do's" to try out an "it could be."

Jochebed's and Pharaoh's daughter's gifts of bravery, creative dreaming and faithfulness to follow through on their dreams give them an essential place in history. It is through these two that God moved and breathed and gave life to Moses and through Moses to the Hebrew people. I wonder what else these two women did in their life time. Did they keep dreaming or did they return to hiding their dreams and desires? What about you? What will you dare to dream? What part of history will you create?

Interpreting the Dream

There is a very delicate balance between enjoying the presence of God in the simple tasks of life, such as dishes, vehicle maintenance, laundry, cooking, cleaning, home repairs, etc. and losing oneself in the tasks. There will always be more than enough "to dos" for you to attend to and in these you can find joy and pursue God. Yet you are called to dream and take action in a unique way. As you consider the following, open yourself to God's light, power and Holy Spirit to speak to you. You may see something you have never seen before or something you have seen but chosen to deny.

On a scale of 1 -10, 1 being not at all and 10 being always, rate with an "X" how much of your God-given identity and joy is visible in what you do in the following areas of your life:

Marriage or significant relationships

| 1 | 2 | 3 | 4 | 5 | 6 | 7 | 8 | 9 | 10 |

Church life/spiritual life

| 1 | 2 | 3 | 4 | 5 | 6 | 7 | 8 | 9 | 10 |

Work life

| 1 | 2 | 3 | 4 | 5 | 6 | 7 | 8 | 9 | 10 |

Family Life

| 1 | 2 | 3 | 4 | 5 | 6 | 7 | 8 | 9 | 10 |

Recreational time

| 1 | 2 | 3 | 4 | 5 | 6 | 7 | 8 | 9 | 10 |

Life Maintenance Duties

| 1 | 2 | 3 | 4 | 5 | 6 | 7 | 8 | 9 | 10 |

Go back through and with an "O" mark how often you dream with God about creating new possibilities in these areas. Notice the difference or the similarities in your markings.

In each of the areas, what is one thing you might dream about with God to increase God's visibility in your life? Try to make these specific. For example, it could be to pursue a specific desire of your heart that you laid down in busyness, having a daily time for prayer, making a trip, taking a course, or … Pick one of these to weave into your life this month.

Dream Walking

Create a dream gallery. Collect magazines with photos. Look through the magazines and ask God to help you identify pictures that demonstrate what God desires to dream with you. See what pictures attract your attention. Be bold and imaginative. God is! When you have finished cutting them out, arrange them on a poster board and hang them where you will see them several times a day. As you focus on these pictures, dream with God about how to make these dreams real. Add to these pictures as new dreams come to you. If you have little wall space, paste the pictures into a file folder. Before and after you have your time with God open the folder and pray over the pictures. The file folder can also stand on a desk or table.

Integrating the Dream

Stand tall with your shoulders back. Put your palms together in front of your chest in the praying hands position. Raise them straight up and then open your hands and arms into a large circle. As you do this, think of yourself opening up to God who is within you.

Daily Prayer Journal

Date _____   Scripture _____

I rejoice in:
      1.
      2.
      3.
      4.
      5.

I hear God saying to me in the scripture:

Faith and visualization statements I am creating with God:

God and I dream about:

I commit to do the following things with God today: (Review the items in this section from yesterday. Are there any you did not complete you want to carry into today's commitments? Review the previous day's list before completing this section each day.)

Day 3

"I was in the city of Joppa praying, and in a trance I saw a vision. There was something like a large sheet coming down from heaven, being lowered by its four corners; and it came close to me." Acts 11:5 NRSV

Reading for the Day: Acts 11

Dreaming: Dream Walking

Imagine a giant sheet coming down from the heavens into your room. On this sheet, you see all kinds of animals that you have been taught were dangerous to eat from the time you were a small child. As you see the animals in the sheet, you back away. What are you feeling?

A voice tells you to "Rise, (your name); kill and eat." You immediately say, "No Lord; for nothing unclean has ever entered my mouth." The voice answers you, "What God has cleansed you must not call unclean." You repeat this dialogue three times. You are told to eat. You refuse. Then comes a sharp reprimand for rejecting what God has made clean for you. Now what are you feeling?

Just as you are trying to process what is happening the sheet is snatched back up into heaven. An opportunity is awaiting you outside the door – three men whom you have considered unclean or perhaps dangerous want your help. What do you do?

This was the vision Peter grappled with long ago. It came to him in the midst of a very heated debate in the church. Should Gentiles be required to convert to Judaism and follow Jewish Law before becoming Christians or not? Before having the vision, Peter fervently believed Gentiles needed to first be made clean by following the Law. Like us, Peter was a product of his upbringing. As a Jewish young person, he had been taught through story and example the importance of the Law in being faithful to God. If he truly loved the Gentiles, how could he possibly not insist they enter into what he knew to be life-saving? This kind of thinking may seem foreign to us. Yet which one of us could be silent with integrity if we believed we knew something that would save another's life? This was Peter's dilemma.

Peter, Paul and the small, but growing church, were trying very hard to understand where they were to lead. Jesus, who himself had followed the Law, had certainly taught them how to pray. He had given them an example to live by and the Holy Spirit to empower them. However, just like today, not all agreed on what God wanted them to do.

In the midst of this very serious debate, Peter, the rock of the church, was given this new vision. What a huge change this had to be in Peter's thinking! As strong as Peter had been in his beliefs prior to the vision, he began to be even more committed to the new truth he now understood – that God could make clean whatever and whomever God wanted in whatever manner God chose. Up until this time, Peter had in a sense been sleep walking in his own beliefs. He did not know what he did not understand. It took a vision, dream walking with God, to open Peter to a new way of thinking and living.

How hard it is sometimes for God to reach us with new ideas and concepts that have not been a part of our culture and upbringing. We somehow need to be jarred into thinking beyond what we have reason to know. Throughout the scriptures, and today as well, God uses the gift of dreams and visions to create insight, change and renewal within us. For the most part, we are familiar and comfortable with dreams. We have them every night. When we pay attention to them, they can often move us to growth. Visions, on the other hand, are like dreams we have when we are awake and they may be more unusual for us.

Just like Peter, we may sometimes drift through life unaware of what we are missing or failing to understand. We may walk and talk and function quite well. However we are missing out on the additional truths God has to share with us. We don't even know what we don't know. For those who are willing to dream just a bit with God, to make ourselves available for visions to come, there is a whole world of possibilities and viewpoints left to see. Dream walking, allowing ourselves to seek deeply what God is dreaming for us and for others, takes us to places and options we never would have found had we continued to only sleep walk.

As a small child you had to slowly learn a vocabulary – first through listening and then through speaking. So, too, with visioning and dreaming, you nurture your ability to listen and to experience by repeatedly practicing dreaming. As you make room in your life to dream and to honor God's guidance in the dreams, their numbers and depth increase.

My husband, Bill, and I have started a practice of dream walking. It is something we do together and separately. As we walk, we ask God to inspire our vision and then acknowledge whatever images come to mind. Sometimes they are funny, other times serious, still at other points our thinking is expanded to imagine that which before was not even a thought we had considered. The more often we exercise our dreaming muscles, the more open in prayer we become to seeing for a moment something new that inspires us to pursue God more fully and deeply.

Dream walking is far more inspiring than sleep walking. For Peter and for us, it gives us the opportunity to grow exponentially in God and to bless those who are touched by our faith and God's spirit within us. What is God leading you to dream today?

Interpreting the Dream

Have you had a dream or vision that has changed the course of your life or actions? Write a little about it and the changes it created in your viewpoint and choices.

If a sheet full of things you reject or fear were to come down from heaven, what would be on it? How does God view the contents of your sheet?

Talk with a friend about a vision or dream that has had meaning to her (him). Did she pursue the dream? What moved her from sleep walking to dream walking, or living out her dream with God?

Have you ever written down your dreams? If so, what was the fruit of this? Put paper and pen by your bed and write down dreams as soon as you wake up. Do this for at least two weeks and see if there are themes of growth there for you to receive. If you have difficulty remembering your dreams, pray before you go to sleep that you will remember and honor the dreams that God gives to you.

Dream Walking

If possible, go for a walk outside today. Ask God to bless you with a real receptivity to God's heart and mind. Then simply walk, listen and acknowledge images or words as they come to you. If you have a spiritual friend or companion, it can be a great experience to walk and speak of these images together. If walking is not an option, sit in silence or with a friend and complete this exercise.

During the day, notice what images come to mind. Be aware of the songs that you may hum. Notice the gentle leadings that come to you. Honor fully God's willingness to be intimately connected with you in partnership and in life. If you are led to speak to someone or take action, step out in faith as you spend the day with God in partnership.

Watch the film, "Glory Road," with friends or on your own. As the characters begin to dream about possibilities how did their lives and the lives of others expand? What were some of the responses to their dream walking?

Amazed at the Standing Stones, Isle of Aran, Scotland
By Thomas C. Russell

Integrating the Dream

Stand tall with your shoulders back. Put your palms together in front of your chest in the praying hands position. Raise them straight up and then open your hands and arms into a large circle. As you do this, think of yourself opening up to God who is within you.

Daily Prayer Journal

Date _____   Scripture _____

I rejoice in:

     1.

     2.

     3.

     4.

     5.

I hear God saying to me in the scripture:

Faith and visualization statements I am creating with God:

God and I dream about:

I commit to do the following things with God today:

Day 4

"We know that all things work together for good for those who love God, who are called according to his purpose." Romans 8:28   NRSV

Reading for the Day: Romans 8:28-39

Dreaming: All Things? Yes, All Things!

When I was in my early years of pastoring, I was frustrated by some of the politics of the church. I mentioned something to my mother on one of our calls and it wasn't long before she brought me a colored glass window with Romans 8:28 written on it. "All things work together for good to those who love the Lord, to those who are called according to God's purpose."

At the time, it seemed like a "nice" gift from my mom. However, the power of this verse has become an increasing encouragement in my life over the years. When things are not as I would have made them, when I am experiencing a challenge that seems too big for me, I seek to see this verse as a promise and a focus for my dreaming.

For me, it does not mean that God has caused these bad things to happen in my life, but rather that God will use whatever happens to create something good if I am open to receiving God's wisdom and insight. Our youngest son, Nate, helped me to understand this. He had no fear of anything. At the church I served, there was a very steep flight of stairs and he would head for them each time he escaped from the nursery. In my parental wisdom, I, or someone else in the church, would always stop him from falling down these and any other stairs. It hit me one day that the best thing I could do for Nate was to let him fall down two relatively small stairs in the front of our house so he could learn about stairs. Now, I did not push him. I was certainly there to dust off his knees and kiss his hurts, but I allowed him to experience stairs and falling. From that day on, he had a greater respect for stairs. Although he still had less fear than I thought was healthy, he had gained some important information about stairs – good came from his falling.

When my mother died of a heart attack, I could see no good in her loss. She was vibrant, wanted to live and had a list of several hundred things she wanted to accomplish during her retirement. The loss of her physical body, the strongest symbol of her we had to embrace, was tremendous. If I could rewrite the story, she would be alive and healthy today. However, as I look back, these are some of the good things that have come from her loss:

My children realize, at some level, that life is not forever and it is worth cherishing.
I am more determined to care for my own health so my children will have a longer time with me if that is God's desire.
My mom did not have to suffer through a lengthy illness or confinement.
In preparing and presiding at funerals since her death, I have far more understanding of those who are grieving.
I am more in touch with the issues facing those who have widowed parents.
At her funeral, I became more fully aware of just how many lives she had touched in her 68 years. She was courageous and chose to make a difference on many occasions. Her life encourages me to be all God calls me to be.

Do all things work together for good? I encourage you to intentionally choose to say "YES!" to this question. As your confidence in Gods grace and power to create good in every situation grows, your courage to dream of possibilities will grow as well. Because you expect God to create good, you will be willing to see and receive the good God has for you. On this belief rests your willingness to dream even in the midst of what may at first appear hopeless. What a gift this promise of God is!

Interpreting the Dream

When something that seems bad happens, often the tendency is to focus on how horrible or unfair it is. A decision is made at some level to feel like a victim in the situation, helpless to create any real change. What would it look like to alter how you view events? What if you could see events as neither good nor bad in and of themselves, but rather as opportunities for God to create good in your life and the lives of others? What would it look like for you to open your arms and your heart to receive whatever happens to you as something that God, in partnership with you, will turn to good? What would this do to your anger? Your desire to blame? Your fear? Your choices? Yur expectations and dreams?

Think for a moment of an event in your life that seemed "bad." Take a moment to remember and feel your experience. If the experience was recent, you will need to imagine the possibilities in this next part. What good can you see coming from this event? What ability or sensitivity or learning do you have now that you did not have before this event? What part of you have you found through this experience?

Who is a person in history, who was experiencing something that seemed devastating to her/him, only to discover the event was the beginning of great things for her/him? What helped these people to dream of possibilities beyond the situation? Did he/she have a sense of trust that good would come?

On a scale of 1 to 10, 1 being not at all and 10 being 100% of the time, how strongly do you believe all things work for good to those who love God? Circle your answer. If you are not yet at a 10, what would it take to increase your faith in this belief?

1	2	3	4	5	6	7	8	9	10

Dream Walking

As you meet the events of your life in the next 24 hours, challenge yourself to see each event as an opportunity, even if at first you want to define it as an obstacle. How does changing your viewpoint change the way you feel? How does it give you new choices? How does believing all things work together for good alter the energy you feel in the game of life? (You may want to put on a small bracelet or perhaps a ring you do not ordinarily wear as a reminder to look for the good.)

Talk with someone today who has been through a difficult time and has found the good in the period of struggle. Ask him/her to talk with you about how they moved through the hardship. What helped him/her to dream again? Did he/she have a sense of trust that good would come?

Read the story, <u>Harold and the Purple Crayon</u>, by Crockett Johnson. What do you hear the story saying to you? Where is your crayon? What color is it? What are you creating?

Integrating the Dream

Stand tall with your shoulders back. Put your palms together in front of your chest in the praying hands position. Raise them straight up and then open your hands and arms into a large circle. As you do this, think of yourself opening up to God who is within you.

⋘⋙⋘⋙⋘⋙⋘⋙⋘⋙⋘⋙⋘⋙⋘⋙⋘⋙⋘⋙⋘⋙⋘⋙⋘⋙⋘⋙⋘⋙

Daily Prayer Journal

Date _____   Scripture _____

I rejoice in:
      1.
      2.
      3.
      4.
      5.

I hear God saying to me in the scripture:

Faith and visualization statements I am creating with God:

God and I dream about:

I commit to do the following things with God today:

⋘⋙⋘⋙⋘⋙⋘⋙⋘⋙⋘⋙⋘⋙⋘⋙⋘⋙⋘⋙⋘⋙⋘⋙⋘⋙⋘⋙⋘⋙

Day 5

"They heard the sound of the LORD God walking in the garden at the time of the evening breeze, and the man and his wife hid themselves from the presence of the LORD God among the trees of the garden." Genesis 3:8 NRSV

Reading for the Day: Genesis 3:1-24

Dreaming: Come Out, Come Out, Wherever You Are!

Travel back with me to the Garden of Eden. You are Eve with Adam and the two of you have eaten from the forbidden fruit. All kinds of new awarenesses are rising up in your minds – we're naked; we're unworthy of God's acceptance; we're seeking for someone to blame for our situation; we're going to die! You talk it over and wish you had not eaten from the tree. What options are you discussing? What are your fears? One of you suggests that you go looking for God and ask for forgiveness. What conversation about this idea do you have? Just as you hear the sound of God coming into the garden, you resist the strong temptation to run and hide. You don't even reach for scratchy fig leaves to cover your naked bodies. As God reaches you, you both kneel down and before God can say a word, you tearfully and hopefully ask to be forgiven. You tell the truth. You each accept responsibility for your choices. Finally you acknowledge that you deserve the punishment of death. You sense God desires so much more for both of you. What does God say? What does God do?

As I dream about this alternative ending, or should I say beginning, I look into my own life and see how I sometimes choose to hide from God when God would so much rather I cry out, "Here I am!" as I go dashing out seeking for God. For some reason, I, just like the original Adam and Eve, grab some scratchy fig leaves and hide from the living God, who in truth knows me better than I do. What would it take for us to understand that God has and will seek us out from our hiding places? When will we realize how deeply God desires us to passionately race out seeking God with all of who we are?

When Adam and Eve chose to eat of the fruit, it kept them from being and doing the infinite number of things God had created for them to experience that would bring them greater life and wholeness. Sometimes we, too, step away from the opportunities we have been blessed with – our talents, our unique personalities, our creativity, our dreams – and instead invest ourselves in that which is not God-driven. Our actions become a thing of shame when God intended for all that we are and do to be a thing of beauty. At some point we may have turned away from the depth of God's desires for us. Perhaps we were told that we weren't wise or funny or beautiful or smart and creative. We believed the serpents that placed these thoughts in our minds. In doing so we hid from our dreams and hopes. Maybe we pretended not to know answers we knew, or we didn't play as hard as we could because someone might be offended, or we stopped smiling and twirling because it was not a grown-up, womanly thing to do and be. As a woman, we didn't speak the words of healing to someone we met because it might appear foolish. We didn't give a life-giving gift because it wasn't practical. We pretended we did not see injustices around us because we felt we could not make a difference.

Like Adam and Eve, we hid when the One who could free us came. Afraid to show our woundedness, our nakedness, our guilt, we jumped into the bushes of life. I wonder if there was some relief for Adam and Eve, even in the midst of their fear of God, that God cared enough to seek them and ask, "Where are you?" God could have chosen to never revisit them after their disobedience. God could have chosen not to ask for them to come out of hiding. But that is not how God is with God's beloved.

In the original story, God began a conversation with Adam and Eve quite similar to one a parent has with a child: What are the facts? Who did what? What are the consequences? And even though Adam and Eve lost access to the garden, they never lost access to the One who chose to seek them even when they did not want to be found.

Throughout creation, God has chosen to find us and be in relationship with us! People like Jacob, Moses, David, Esther, Paul and many more hid from God. Yet God's love for them and for us abounds. Each one of these people eventually stepped forward and found their faith and their extraordinariness in God. Yes, they all faltered again. However they seemed to grow in their trust of God. They did not always hide and wait for God to find them. They learned to pursue God and who God created them to be, even when they felt unworthy. For those of us born after the coming of Jesus, we have been given an amazing gift of seeing in his life the clear promise of God's willingness to give even God's own son that we might realize God desires to love us and be in partnership with us, no matter what we have done. What greater reason to come out of hiding and accept our calling?

Have you ever chosen to hide from who God has created you to be? Or have you hidden from full participation in the game of life with God? When you hide behind resentment, God chooses to find you and call you out with, "Come out, come out, wherever you are! You do not need to stay in that place of negativity; come to base and start over!" When you hide behind confusion, attempting nothing and justifying it because you are confused, God cries out to you, "Come out, come out, wherever you are." God shows you how to begin the game of life anew. When you hide behind a belief in scarcity where there is not enough for everyone, God calls you out and proclaims the good news that there is room for all those who wish to respond to the call.

Whatever you may have been hiding from God – your greatness, a sin, a fear, a hope for the extraordinary – God is coming to you today and saying, "Where are you?" Are you willing to play the game of discovery full out as you did when you were a child? Are you ready to laugh and run with delight even when you may "lose" a round knowing that the game is far more than any one play? Are you ready to trust God enough to cry out, "Here I am!"

In 2 Corinthians 13:14, Paul writes to the Corinthians, "The grace of the Lord Jesus Christ and the love of God and the fellowship of the Holy Spirit be with you all." RSV Are you ready to fully participate? Are you ready to be a partner with God choosing to find the new discoveries God has for you? The journey will not always be comfortable. Sometimes God will reveal to you things you may rather not see. God will challenge you to come out in ways you have never tried. Yet God will always be there, desiring to be found by you and at times searching for you. God will always be ready to embrace you as you love and live together.

You are God's beloved! You and the dreams God has placed in your heart are worthy of being found. "Ready or not, here you come!"

Interpreting the Dream

Do I believe God is really seeking me? Do I trust that God loves me so much that God would do whatever it takes to find me?

List some ways you hide from God in your life.

What would it take for me to believe it is safe for me to search for God wholeheartedly?

Describe a time when you feel like God found you. What did you experience? What did you feel? Did you grow from the experience?

Describe a time when you feel like you searched for God. What did you do? Where did you go? What was your experience?

Dream Walking

In the game of Hide and Seek, when "It" shouts, "Ready or not, here I come," she eagerly runs out seeking all those who are in hiding. As you live your day today, intentionally seek out God. Where is God working? How is God working with the child down the street? In what way is God present at a city council meeting? How is God with the driver who is next to you in traffic? Really be with God today. Acknowledge God in others and in yourself. Share with God what you are thinking and feeling. What are your joys and fears?

Pick one thing to do today that you normally would not do because you see God at work there. Perhaps you will invent something, visit someone who is grieving, invest in a new project, or … Choose to be where God is at work and go with joy and power as one who has been chosen to be a daughter of God.

Integrating the Dream

Stand tall with your shoulders back. Put your palms together in front of your chest in the praying hands position. Raise them straight up and then open your hands and arms into a large circle. As you do this, think of yourself opening up to God who is within you.

Daily Prayer Journal

Date _____   Scripture _____

I rejoice in:
       1.
       2.
       3.
       4.
       5.

I hear God saying to me in the scripture:

Faith and visualization statements I am creating with God:

God and I dream about:

I commit to do the following things with God today:

Woman Smiling
By Holly C. Rudolf

Day 6

"The Lord GOD has given me the tongue of a teacher, that I may know how to sustain the weary with a word. Morning by morning he wakens—wakens my ear to listen as those who are taught." Isaiah 50:4 NRSV

Reading for the Day: Isaiah 50:1-11

Dreaming: It's Time to Go!

Lois, a friend in her late 80's, was healing from a broken hip. She seemed to be on the mend and was talking about returning to her daily golf game. Just before being released from the hospital, she had a heart attack. As the doctors and nurses attended her, she confidently said, "Time to go!" Her eyes closed for the last time and she began the next chapter of life with God. Her family retold that story to me and I have retold it to many others. Lois' words were just the right ones to help her family and friends let go of her physical body and send her on her way with a tear and a smile.

I doubt Lois was thinking consciously about those who loved her and how they would accept or understand her death. Yet somehow she intuited what was needed by us and chose to speak those words as her last. She could have "heard" the pain in her chest and commented on that. She could have listened to the noises around her. Yet she chose to focus on what she could "hear" in a greater way. What a comfort to those of us not yet at death's doorstep to listen to her confidence and even matter-of-factness as she moved on down the road. Lois' mouth and ears sustained the weary.

A family stood in shock around a loved one in a coma in an emergency room. A swift heart attack had taken their loved one from consciousness to silence in a moment's time. The minister entered the room just as the family was beginning to pray. They turned to him to speak the words. His words were very simple and clear. "May God's circle of love and care surround you." His prayer comforted the family and brought a strong sense of God's presence into the room. He heard the family's need and spoke the words that sustained them.

A two-year-old child saw his grandpa sitting and weeping. Without hesitating, the child walked to him and wiggled gently into his lap. "I love you," said the child. His grandpa embraced the child and sobbed gently until, with the child wiping away his tears, he began to smile. The child "heard" what was being spoken and said the words that were needed to bring life and hope.

How blessed Isaiah was to feel that his tongue had actually been taught to sustain another who was weary, even someone who tormented him. How wonderful that he understood the connection between having a "learned tongue" and ears trained to hear and understand. Ears that not only heard the words that were spoken, but also the need, the hope, the desire and, yes, the God-given dreams of those he met.

Imagine for a moment a world in which you really heard what another was saying before you spoke. Imagine what might be if your words were truly trained and designed to sustain another. Imagine the gift of being heard before being spoken to. What might happen in your home? Your neighborhood? Your world?

May you be blessed to feel God awaken you each morning with the gift of learned ears and a tongue that matches them.

Interpreting the Dream

Remember a time when your words were harsh and discouraging to someone else. Who was the person? What was the situation? How were you feeling before and after you spoke? What were the short term results for the person you spoke to that day? What were the short term results for you? Were there things in your life or this person's life that were different months or even years down the road because of this event?

Remember a time when your words encouraged someone else to pursue excellence and greater possibilities. Who was the person? What was the situation? What feeling did you have as you began to speak? What were the short term results for the person you spoke to that day? What were the short term results for you? Were there things in your life or this person's life that were different months or even years down the road because of this event?

Dream Walking

Today, be attentive to the power of your words. When you speak, notice the way people respond. Do your words bring life, encouragement and hope? Do your words inspire those you meet to dream? For today, choose to speak to at least three people in a way that will honestly address them as precious children of God with an important part to play in the world.

Be attentive to the words you speak to yourself. What do your words do for you? What words would God desire you to speak into your own life?

May your words sustain and encourage you and others to step out a little further into God's dreams.

Integrating the Dream

Stand tall with your shoulders back. Put your palms together in front of your chest in the praying hands position. Raise them straight up and then open your hands and arms into a large circle. As you do this, think of yourself opening up to God who is within you.

Daily Prayer Journal

Date _____   Scripture _____

I rejoice in:
    1.
    2.
    3.
    4.
    5.

I hear God saying to me in the scripture:

Faith and visualization statements I am creating with God:

God and I dream about:

I commit to do the following things with God today:

Day 7

"Then Jesus turned round and said to Peter, 'Out of my way, Satan! . . . You stand right in my path, Peter, when you look at things from man's point of view and not from God's.'" Matthew 16:23 J.B. Phillips Translation

Reading for the Day: Matthew 16:13-28

Dreaming: Whose Side Are You Leaning On?

How far are we willing to stretch ourselves as we dream with God? Are we willing to imagine and to step into dreams we at first do not understand or trust?

Peter was so close to Christ. He even knew at some level Jesus was "the Christ, the Son of the living God." (Matthew 16:16 RSV) Yet when Jesus began to talk to the disciples about his suffering and death, it was too much for Peter! How could Jesus possibly think God would allow him to die like that? What would be gained?

Dismayed by Jesus' words, I imagine Peter went to Jesus and gently pulled him aside. Perhaps the master had just been preaching and teaching too long and needed a rest. He knew he could help Jesus see all this talk about going to Jerusalem was crazy. The world obviously needed Jesus to live so he could preach and teach and heal. How could Jesus even think dying was his destiny?

Jesus was not persuaded. His words to Peter were some of the harshest he ever spoke. Jesus knew that he was living out the dream he was called to live. He understood that his death and resurrection would bring great life, forgiveness and faith for generations to come. He was a part of God's dream, a dream that included every person seeing an incredible visible sign that God's love and grace are freely given to all.

Jesus also knew he could not afford to have those closest to him encouraging him to deny God's dream for him. He needed to guard himself from those who would take away the dream that God had birthed him to fulfill. Jesus knew from his time of temptation (Luke 4:1-13) that there are many possible dreams to pursue. Many are even good dreams. Yet Jesus knew deep within himself that only those dreams embedded in God and God's desires are worthy of living out with all he had to give. He was determined to dream walk with God and to go far beyond what others thought was wise or prudent. He could not allow Peter, or anyone, to dissuade him.

Jesus shared many dreams with God during his life on earth. Some led him to sit and talk with small children. In others, he was gifted with the power to heal and forgive. There were even dreams he shared with God as he participated in worship and weddings and the everyday events of eating and sleeping. Jesus' ending dream on earth was not an easy one. He was more than willing for God to choose another path for him. However, when he was certain of his calling, he gave everything he had to pursue the dream.

Sometimes as you dream with God, you will also find yourself led onto difficult paths. Like Peter, you may want to rewrite the dream, to hear a different story. It may take everything you have to push yourself to dream beyond what is comfortable to what is God-sized and yes, miraculous. If you really want to dream big with God, it will require you to stretch. It will be absolutely essential that you surround yourself with people who will help you dream and encourage you to remain faithful to your calling. You will need to pray fervently, especially when you enter new territories. You can be confident, that as you are faithful in pursuing dream walking with God, your dreams will multiply and increase. God will trust you with more and more of God's dreams. Your sensitivities will grow and you will sense God's presence in more and more of who you are and what you do.

The pursuit of dreaming into the depths of God's dreams for you will require you to move beyond your own desires and understanding. May you have the courage to stretch your heart and mind so that you might dream freely and openly with God.

Interpreting the Dream

Rewrite today's scripture. Peter obviously knew how to pursue God's dreams for him. He had left all he had to follow Jesus. However, when Jesus revealed his destiny, Peter was not able to dream the dream Jesus was sharing. If Peter were open to dream walking with God in this situation, what might he have said to Jesus? What might he have done?

Through this first week, you have been asked to open yourself to seek for the dreams God has placed in your heart. You have been recording and honoring your dreams. Have you found some areas of your life in which you are sleep walking? Are there areas where you, like Peter in today's story, are resisting dreaming and following God?

List three people who mentor or encourage you to pursue God's dreams.
1.
2.
3.

Describe one of these people and how they support you in dreaming with God. What are some specific things they say or do? How do they interact with you?

Which of God's dreams are you pursuing? What is supporting you? What is hindering you? What step will you take today to pursue your dreams with God?

Dream Walking

Talk with someone who is pursuing a dream with God at full tilt. If no one is available, read about Mother Teresa in a book or on the internet. What has called her/him to this dream? What or who has kept her/him in strong pursuit of the dream?

If you are clear about a part of the dream walking God is calling you to do, write it down and share it with at least one person. Ask him or her to hold you accountable for pursuing your God-given dreams. This might be something you do for each other.

Consider for a moment the people God has placed in your life. Who could you mentor or encourage to dream God's dreams? Select three women you could intentionally encourage. List them.
1.
2.
3.

Look back at "Interpreting the Dream" at the specific ways people have encouraged you. Which of these might be ones you could use to encourage the three women you have chosen to intentionally support? Imagine what God could do through you if you mentored and encouraged three women, who encouraged three women, who encouraged…How amazing it could be!

Integrating the Dream

Stand tall with your shoulders back. Put your palms together in front of your chest in the praying hands position. Raise them straight up and then open your hands and arms into a large circle. As you do this, think of yourself opening up to God who is within you.

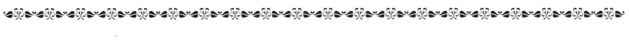

Daily Prayer Journal

Date _____   Scripture _____

I rejoice in:

      1.

      2.

      3.

      4.

      5.

I hear God saying to me in the scripture:

Faith and visualization statements I am creating with God:

God and I dream about:

I commit to do the following things with God today:

Day 8

"Therefore, since we are surrounded by so great a cloud of witnesses, let us also lay aside every weight and the sin that clings so closely, and let us run with perseverance the race that is set before us, looking to Jesus the pioneer and perfecter of our faith, who for the sake of the joy that was set before him endured the cross, disregarding its shame, and has taken his seat at the right hand of the throne of God. Consider him who endured such hostility against himself from sinners, so that you may not grow weary or lose heart." Hebrews 12:1-3 NRSV

Reading for the Day: Hebrews 11:1 – Hebrews 12:1-29

Dreaming: Who Sits at Your Table?

When your family gets together, how do you decide where everyone sits? In my family growing up, who you sat next to was determined by age. Younger people sat at the smaller table on piano benches and everyday chairs. Adults sat at the big table with the carved wooden chairs. Depending on how many of the family came to the event, people might shift from table to table.

At one point when I was focused on someone with whom I had a conflict, my husband asked me, "Why would you bring her home with you?" Now I had not physically brought her into our home, but he was right. I was entertaining her many hours a day in my mind. I had brought her to sit at my table. I chose to dine with her rather than to dine with people I would truly enjoy. I did not even bring the best parts of her to the table. Rather, I brought the most negative experiences of her into my mind. My energy and creative thinking were wrapped around her. All the time, I could have been focused on imagining people sitting with me who were humorous, encouraging or helpful in stretching my thinking, but I chose not to do so.

How do you decide who sits at the tables you host within your mind? Who do you entertain in your mind when their physical presence may not even be near you? Who sits at the big table? Who sits at a smaller table removed a bit from the center of your attention? People you have known, wish that you had known and some people that you have created along the way all exist in your mind. The question is, at which table do you allow them to dine? How often are they your guests? Do you decide the topic of conversation and set the boundaries of what is appropriate and inappropriate?

Just like you choose who you will invite to your home, you have a choice about who eats at the table of your mind and heart. You can bring people who cause you to grow and stretch. You can ponder people with incredible faith to inspire you. You can even meditate on people who have the spiritual gifts and talents you are seeking or developing.

I am more and more selective of the guests I allow at the table of my mind. I value my time too much to pick up after those who are unnecessarily messy. When I am selective, I find my energy and creativity increase. When I bring those to the table of my mind who are negative or hurtful, it only wounds me.

Hebrews 12:1 reminds us that we are surrounded by a huge cloud of witnesses all the time. Most of Hebrews 11 is a list of some of these witnesses. Today as you interact with one other person and touch her/him with a bit of God's grace and power, pretend this cloud of witnesses is sitting at your table and begins to clap for you. Imagine they shout words of encouragement joyfully to you, ideas for the next step and even laugh with delight as you and the person you are speaking with experience God more deeply in the moment.

God has indeed given you a great cloud of witnesses. If you will listen for them, they can and will encourage and guide you. In your imaginary conversations with them, you may even find the keys to solutions you are seeking.

Sometimes when I get stuck and I am not sure which direction to head, I imagine the cloud of witnesses as specific individuals. I think of Jesus, my mother, Lydia in Acts 16, Maya Angelou and Jimmy Carter. I invite them to the table of my mind and together we have a conversation about the issue that concerns me. Sometimes imagining their words stirs my heart to hear God's voice in ways I was missing. Sometimes it causes me to see the humor in the situation. Seeing the world through their eyes brings me closer to God and God's ways.

Now, I realize that I can't know for sure what they would think or say. However, by allowing my mind to dwell on their lives and how they faced many challenges, I bring to my mind the opportunity to dwell in that which is good, holy, sacred, creative and positive. What a gift to focus on those who have done so much with God! My mind and your mind are powerful things. They can bring us closer to God and to God-sized opportunities or they can drag us into defeat, negativism and fear.

I choose to decide who I will bring to my table. I will dine with those who bring me closer to the One who has set the feast before us. What about you?

Interpreting the Dream

Consider the people you find yourself thinking about during a typical week. List them. Circle the ones who are guests you intentionally choose to "dine" with you as you seek to create a strong, healthy mind in God.

Do you allow yourself to sit at the adult table in your mind? Are you always at the children's table while others take the seats at the adult table? Is there anyone God is calling you to dine with as one adult with another adult?

Name some women and men who are spiritual giants in your eyes. Think about the talents and experiences each one has/had that you admire. List the person and the traits.

Review your answers. Pick a council of four or five people you believe would be strong witnesses to you of the presence of God at work in your life.

Dream Walking

Pick one person from your list and throughout the day - perhaps when a phone rings, you check email, or you tend to the needs of a child - imagine them clapping for you and encouraging you to pursue your dreams with God today.

Imagine you are sitting at a dining room table. You have three seats plus your own. Invite three guests to your imaginary table and have a discussion with them about a topic of your choice. Consider repeating this exercise as you make decisions and dream with God. Sometimes when you seek to view things from a different person's perspective, it creates a freedom to dream in new ways.

If you find yourself bringing people to the table of your mind who are discouraging or upsetting you, consciously choose to ask them to leave the table. Invite one of your honored guests to come and bring light and possibilities to your mind. Your table belongs to you. You have the power to choose who will dine with you.

Listen to the song, "You Raise Me Up," by Josh Groban, as you sit or lie in a relaxed state. Visualize God or one of these witnesses raising you up to fulfill the dreams you are created to live.

Integrating the Dream

It is essential that you replace thinking that is detrimental to your dreaming with think-ing that builds your desire and ability to dream. Notice if you find yourself choosing to think or feel something which stops you from dreaming and walking with God in faith. If you do, place your hand up to your throat as if you were going to choke your-self. Be sure not to apply pressure. This quick physical reminder is a warning to you that this type of thinking chokes the very life and spirit from you. Now move your hand from your throat to your heart. Allow yourself to refill your mind with God's dreams for you. Be sure to refocus your thinking on a portion of a dream or statement of blessing that is important to you. Actively choose life and dreaming.

Consider asking someone close to you to join you in this activity. If either of you becomes aware the conversation is detrimental to dreaming and living life fully, the choking signal is done and followed by moving the hand to the heart. This partnership can help to reveal some thought patterns that may be so familiar to you that you do not initially see them for yourself. It can also add a touch of humor and hope to the process of reshaping your thinking.

Daily Prayer Journal

Date _____   Scripture _____

I rejoice in:
     1.
     2.
     3.
     4.
     5.

I hear God saying to me in the scripture:

Faith and visualization statements I am creating with God:

God and I dream about:

I commit to do the following things with God today: (Review your first week of commitments. How well are you completing these? Are there any you missed you want to move to today's list?)

Day 9

"He woke up and rebuked the wind, and said to the sea, 'Peace! Be still!' Then the wind ceased, and there was a dead calm." Mark 4:39 NRSV

Reading for the Day: Mark 4:35-41

Dreaming: Peace! Be Still!

There was a storm today. Not the kind that blows and pelts rain at you from the sky, but the kind of storm that comes when people disagree strongly about things that are important to them. I, of course, was right. The mother always is, you know. Yet I somehow found myself wanting to rain down judgments and consequences from on high in the midst of the debate. How could my son not see the love and wisdom in my words? How could he not understand the gift of being a part of this family in this moment? I was angry and then hurt. Then came frustration and weariness. Then, of course, guilt and challenges to myself about what I could do better.

The storm was raging, at least within me, even though we went to separate places agreeing to disagree for now. What do I do with the storm, Lord? Are you sleeping? Can I wake you up? I wonder about how you calmed the storm for the disciples with a command, "Peace! Be still!" You weren't angry at the storm or eager to judge. You simply stopped it. How clear cut and easy. It was all so obvious. You questioned the disciples, "Why are you afraid? Do you still have no faith?" Are you questioning me, too, Lord?

This son you gave me has so many ideas of his own. He is so clear about what is right and wrong, what is fair and what is not fair, what is fun and what is drudgery. Lord, help me to calm the storm within me so that I, too, can be clear on the boundaries, yet not judging of the storm itself. You were not angry that the storm was the storm. Who knows, perhaps you even prayed for rain to heal the land before you went to sleep to rest in faith? Help me to truly bless the best that is in my son –the one you gave to me with such love and trust. For the storm within me becomes still as I realize that I do have the power to bless him and to guide him – not control him – but to truly bless him and envision him being the man of God you have created him to be.

I am much too quick to judge the things that I fear or don't understand. Help me, God, to calm the storm of judgment within me and to call for a blessing on all that is good in myself and others. The person who cuts me off in traffic, the family who seems to have everything "all together," the political candidates that never stop campaigning, the suffering of illness in my father, the person who deals unjustly with me in business…help me to be quiet and still within myself. Help me to call forth in prayer the good that could be in them and in me. Grant me the gift, Lord, of praying for them and in so doing still the storm within me.

You, Lord, amaze me. How tired you must have been when they woke you. Yet you cared for their needs and you called them to greater faith. No wonder they were astounded. Your relationship and love for them continued even in the midst of them disappointing you. You do this for me, too, Lord. When I begin to feel as though I am surrounded by a storm, quiet me and call forth from me the blessing you have placed within me. May I not need to cry out for you so many times. Help me to proclaim the words of faith that can calm storms and bring forth the possibilities you desire to be in me and in others.

Interpreting the Dream

Where do waves threaten your peace of mind? Take a look at each of these and ask for a blessing for this person or event. As you do so you open up new pathways for making strong connections that bring greater life to you and to the situation.

Is there something that would help you to remember to calm the storm and bless the situation throughout your days? This could be a small stone in a pocket, a bracelet, a picture, or other item. When you choose to claim the peace and seek the blessing consistently in your life for 30 days, you will see new opportunities open for you and for those you touch.

Dream Walking

Give yourself permission to greet any storm with the knowledge that Christ is with you. Imagine Christ is saying with you, "Peace! Be still!" Imagine what blessing Christ would desire to place on the situation or person. Say this blessing with Christ.

Integrating the Dream

It is essential that you replace thinking that is detrimental to your dreaming with thinking that builds your desire and ability to dream. Notice if you find yourself choosing to think or feel something which stops you from dreaming and walking with God in faith. If you do, place your hand up to your throat as if you were going to choke yourself. Be sure <u>not</u> to apply pressure. This quick physical reminder is a warning to you that this type of thinking chokes the very life and spirit from you. Now move your hand from your throat to your heart. Allow yourself to refill your mind with God's dreams for you. Be sure to refocus your thinking on a portion of a dream or statement of blessing that is important to you. Actively choose life and dreaming.

Consider asking someone close to you to join you in this activity. If either of you becomes aware the conversation is detrimental to dreaming and living life fully, the choking signal is done and followed by moving the hand to the heart. This partnership can help to reveal some thought patterns that may be so familiar to you that you do not initially see them for yourself. It can also add a touch of humor and hope to the process of reshaping your thinking.

Daily Prayer Journal

Date _____   Scripture _____

I rejoice in:
     1.
     2.
     3.
     4.
     5.

I hear God saying to me in the scripture:

Faith and visualization statements I am creating with God:

God and I dream about:

I commit to do the following things with God today:

Coins Flowing from Ewer in Tel Aviv, Israel Museum
By Holly C. Rudolf

Day 10

"He who supplies seed to the sower and bread for food will supply and multiply your seed for sowing and increase the harvest of your righteousness. You will be enriched in every way for your great generosity, which will produce thanksgiving to God through us;" 2 Corinthians 9:10, 11 NRSV

Reading for the Day: 2 Corinthians 9:1-15

Dreaming: To Give or Not to Give, That is the Question – Or Is It?

When I was a young teen, my parents got up in church to give the stewardship testimonial during the annual pledge drive. I truly did not have a clue what they would say. My parents had always quietly and consistently written checks to the church and given us money for the offering plate, but I didn't really know what was at the heart of their discipline of giving. I had "overheard" the two of them talking the night before, not quite sure what they should share with others.

I sat in the balcony with my friends waiting for my mom to start. I wasn't expecting anything too deep or long and yet I saw on her face and on my father's a vulnerability and determination that was unique. Then the story began. My mother described how she had been taught from the time she was a very small girl to tithe. It didn't matter if the harvest was good or bad, if she and my aunt needed shoes or not, her parents simply tithed. I imagine that my grandfather, Ralph Gasche, who homesteaded in Finney County, Kansas, must have even tithed during the years he broke ground and lived in a sod house, waiting for the day he could bring his beloved safely to her new home. My mom talked about falling in love with my dad and how the two of them went on a "date" to church. (I knew something was terribly wrong with her concept of dating at that point!) When my father put in his weekly dime (this was in the 1940's), my mother knew they had a big problem. That very day they discussed tithing and my mother was able to show my dad how important it was to her and to her faith. I imagine being in love with her didn't hurt my dad's desire to please her either, yet in tithing my dad began to develop a new sense of stewardship. It became a partnership between him, my mom and God.

After they married, they struggled to make ends meet and to buy their first home. They even ate cereal – lots of it according to my dad – to get a set of dishes. In those first few years, my mother's medical condition was difficult and they lost a baby early in pregnancy. They finally discovered that my mother's lower back had never been fused together properly and not only would she be unable to carry a child, she would also most likely lose her ability to walk in a few years. In fact, the doctors were not really certain how she had walked all the years she had. They had a choice – surgery or a wheel chair and no children. Knowing my mother could be paralyzed or even die during the operation, they made the decision to have surgery.

A few days after her surgery, the minister came to visit. My mother was still critical and they would not know for several weeks if she could walk. My father, who has been blind since birth, handed the minister the checkbook and asked him to write a check to the church for him to sign. The minister urged him to keep the checkbook and not worry about giving to the church with all the concerns and financial burdens they had.

My father cleared his throat and handed the minister the checkbook again with these words, "We are tithers and this is no time to stop tithing now." Quietly, the minister wrote the check and helped my dad to sign it.

Through joy and in sorrow, through sickness and in health, my father had created a discipline of giving. It wasn't so much the giving that counted to him, it was the honoring of his partnership with God and with my mother. No, my father did not expect his gift would guarantee my mother would walk or even live. He did not assume giving would assure him that they would have the children they wanted. He simply knew from experience that the more he sowed in this partnership, the more fruit of all kinds would naturally flow. He could trust God to supply his real needs. Although he knew little of what would happen in the future, he knew he could trust in the One who created both him and my mother.

Come to think of it, it really isn't about giving. It's about trust in our partnership with the One who truly does supply seed to the sower. It is about relying on the One who will multiply our resources and increase our harvest of righteousness. It is about trusting God to supply us with all we need as we seek to pursue the dreams God has placed in our hearts.

Can you truly trust the One who has given you life? What are you willing to give as you dream with God?

Interpreting the Dream

What is your current discipline of giving?

The Hebrew people used to dance joyfully as they brought their offerings to the altar. What are the feelings you connect to giving?

Are there ways in which God is asking you to give differently?

How does God multiply your giving right now? How is it used in your partnership dreaming with God?

Dream Walking

As you journey through the day, give thanks to God for the gifts you receive. Experience the joy of gratitude. Notice the opportunities you have to give in God's name. Give thanks for God trusting you in this partnership and for the dreams that bloom through your giving.

Integrating the Dream

It is essential that you replace thinking that is detrimental to your dreaming with thinking that builds your desire and ability to dream. Notice if you find yourself choosing to think or feel something which stops you from dreaming and walking with God in faith. If you do, place your hand up to your throat as if you were going to choke yourself. Be sure <u>not</u> to apply pressure. This quick physical reminder is a warning to you that this type of thinking chokes the very life and spirit from you. Now move your hand from your throat to your heart. Allow yourself to refill your mind with God's dreams for you. Be sure to refocus your thinking on a portion of a dream or statement of blessing that is important to you. Actively choose life and dreaming.

Consider asking someone close to you to join you in this activity. If either of you becomes aware the conversation is detrimental to dreaming and living life fully, the choking signal is done and followed by moving the hand to the heart. This partnership can help to reveal some thought patterns that may be so familiar to you that you do not initially see them for yourself. It can also add a touch of humor and hope to the process of reshaping your thinking.

Daily Prayer Journal

Date _____   Scripture _____

I rejoice in:
1.
2.
3.
4.
5.

I hear God saying to me in the scripture:

Faith and visualization statements I am creating with God:

God and I dream about:

I commit to do the following things with God today:

Day 11

"Then Joshua said to Achan, 'My son, give glory to the LORD God of Israel and make confession to him. Tell me now what you have done; do not hide it from me.'" Joshua 7:19 NRSV

Reading for the Day: Joshua 7:1-26

Dreaming: Hiding from Sin

Today's passage is not an easy read for us. In modern ethics, we do not punish an entire family for an individual's crime. We certainly do not take a whole family out and stone and burn them. However, we must remember that justice in Achan's time was different than ours. What is it that this story has to tell us about sin today?

When Achan chose to break faith and disobey the command to leave behind the spoils, he was not thinking of those his sin would affect. He did not consider more than his immediate desire. He finally confessed, but only after his name was drawn out by lot. How long would he have been willing to hold onto the items while the people searched for the one who had broken the agreement with God?

As I ponder this passage, it seems so simple to me that Achan should not have taken things. Wasn't there someone, a friend, a wife, a son, who saw him and could counsel him against such an act? Just how long did Achan think he could hide his sin? Wouldn't he eventually take the items out and show them to someone or sell them? Achan seemed so unaware of the short-term or long-term consequences of his actions. What did his wife and children feel as they were dragged out to their deaths? Was Achan's sin really worth the price he and others paid?

It is easy for me to judge Achan. As I pray over this passage, I realize I should thank him for helping me to see a part of my own sin. I have taken what was not mine. I have hidden that which God desired me not to take from the spoils of life. I have clung to anger, resentment, negativity, fear, shame and doubt. I have stored them in my tent as if they were treasures. I got them out when no one was looking. I valued them as signs of my pain, suffering and victimization. I have used energy tending to them, keeping them safe, when I could have been out winning great victories with God.

What has been the cost of treasuring these sins? Less joy to share with my family and friends. Less hope, less forgiveness, less energy, less triumphs, less of what God has desired me to be. Have I not caused myself and them to be less protected? And yes, those I love the most, my husband and children, have in a sense died with me when I have refused to stop holding onto these things. They have suffered because of my inability to ask for forgiveness and to receive grace as I let go of all things that are not true treasures in my love relationship with God. The pile of stones which was heaped over Achan and his family has heaped over mine as well. And when I have lost my joy in God I have caused my family to feel and bear the stones that I attracted to myself in despair.

Are you also like Achan? Yes, your world is different and certainly your understanding of forgiveness is different, but are you like him? Have you taken something that God knew would not bring you life? What have you hidden within your tent that needs to be released and returned?

It is wise to review what you are hiding from yourself and from God periodically. How subtly some things slide from our view. God is strong enough and loving enough to forgive you and guide you, if you are willing to let your "treasures" go.

Interpreting the Dream

Is there sin which is keeping you and your family from enjoying dreaming with God? What are you hiding? We are clearly told in scripture that "all have sinned and fall short of the glory of God." (Romans 3:23 RSV) In Christ we are clear that there is forgiveness and this is a huge blessing! All we need do is give our sin up to God. So simple to do, and yet so easy not to do. In two minutes or less, list what sins are hidden in your tent. What is keeping you from the fullness of your love relationship with God? These could be past experiences, choices, thinking patterns or emotions that you find yourself returning to over and over again instead of living in the present.

Pick one of these for today and visualize yourself giving this to God. *See Appendix A for help in beginning visualization if you are not accustomed to visualizing.* Imagine you and God talking and replacing that sin with a visual image or activity that brings you closer to God. For example, if you struggle with resentment, explore replacing this by claiming, seeing and naming the experience of gratitude. Today when you start to hold onto the "treasure" that you have hidden, visually replace it with a life-giving treasure from God that never needs to be hidden. Its value will truly bring you and those you touch fullness of life in God.

Dream Walking

Intentionally tend your thoughts today. If you try to pick back up a sin you have given to God, gently stop and visually give it back to God. Replace the thought with the thought of receiving forgiveness, grace and transformation.

Integrating the Dream

It is essential that you replace thinking that is detrimental to your dreaming with thinking that builds your desire and ability to dream. Notice if you find yourself choosing to think or feel something which stops you from dreaming and walking with God in faith. If you do, place your hand up to your throat as if you were going to choke yourself. Be sure not to apply pressure. This quick physical reminder is a warning to you that this type of thinking chokes the very life and spirit from you. Now move your hand from your throat to your heart. Allow yourself to refill your mind with God's dreams for you. Be sure to refocus your thinking on a portion of a dream or statement of blessing that is important to you. Actively choose life and dreaming.

Consider asking someone close to you to join you in this activity. If either of you becomes aware the conversation is detrimental to dreaming and living life fully, the choking signal is done and followed by moving the hand to the heart. This partnership can help to reveal some thought patterns that may be so familiar to you that you do not initially see them for yourself. It can also add a touch of humor and hope to the process of reshaping your thinking.

Daily Prayer Journal

Date _____   Scripture _____

I rejoice in:
      1.
      2.
      3.
      4.
      5.

I hear God saying to me in the scripture:

Faith and visualization statements I am creating with God:

God and I dream about:

I commit to do the following things with God today:

Day 12

"Honor your father and your mother, that your days may be long in the land which the Lord your God gives you." Exodus 20:12 RSV

Reading for the Day: Exodus 20:1-20

Dreaming: How Did I Become the "They" I Used to Talk About?

Have you ever looked into a mirror and wondered how you had strangely morphed into one of those adults you used to talk about? How did it happen? Where did the time and your coolness go?

Today I stood in a doctor's office. I was with my father, who is 87 years old and I was hovering over him as my mother and her sister used to hover over their mother. I wanted to be sure that all the questions were asked and all the options were considered that would give him the greatest health and quality of life. I worried over him as he once worried over me. When we went to lunch afterwards, he reminded me of the times he didn't quite know what would happen to me – the year I changed colleges twice, the time I went vagabonding for a year in my red and black 1971 Maverick, the time… I had to smile as he reminded me how glad he and my mother were each time I came back to my senses.

I have become my mother, my father. My mother, now with God for over 15 years, surely looks at me and smiles as she remembers. She thinks of the times I did not understand why she prayed so hard for all of her children. Now it seems quite obvious as I pray for our children and the wisdom to raise them. She remembers the times I used my young sarcasm to dishonor her beliefs and concerns and now I can't understand how my children sometimes fail to see how awesome my thoughts are and how blessed they are to have me for a mom. And, yes, she also sees the times I have honored her and my father by carrying on the best of who she was and who my father is. The times I sing to my children. The times when I encourage someone to go just one step further because I know they can do so. The opportunities I have utilized to protect or shield the least of these until they became strong. Yes, I have become my mother and my father and, by doing so, I am honoring them in a new way, through my own life and purpose.

This commandment to honor my parents has become richer for me as it is now my father who sometimes needs me. Honoring my father means slowing the world down and going to a doctor's visit with him. It means interpreting the things that go by him too quickly. It means reminding him he still has so much to give.

Honoring my parents means I now understand why my mother would occasionally get out my grandfather's picture and cry. I used to ask her why and she would simply say through tear-streaked cheeks, "I miss him." I didn't understand, but now I do.

My parents were not perfect and honoring them does not require I forget that. It does mean claiming all the things they did exceedingly well and being sure I carry on the inheritance given to them by God and shared with me. Things like truthfulness, for-giveness, endurance, persistent prayer, loving even when it is not easy and pursuing hope, are all gifts I will carry with me and honor in them. I pray that my children will also honor these in me one day.

Yes, I look into the mirror and I see that I am one of "them." I cannot hide from it, nor do I choose to do so. As I dream today it is as one who is no longer a child, but one who has journeyed through life gleaning wisdom and experiences along the way. By carrying the best with me of all those I have known, my dreaming is more fluid and full. It is more hopeful and promising because I choose to honor the best of what has been and carry it into the future with me.

It is my privilege to honor my parents. It is in honoring them that I find I am closer to God and to the woman God is creating me to be. Is this why, God, you commanded me to honor them and to claim what was beautiful in them? Not so much for them only, but for me as well, that I would choose to be a living memorial to them and to You? Help me, God, to honor You and them in all I say and do this day.

Who do you see when you look into the mirror?

Interpreting the Dream

Take time to study yourself in a mirror. Who do you see?

List the characteristics of your mother and father that were God or life honoring. If your parents were not believers, what were some of the things God was able to teach you through them? If your parents were abusive, finding honorable traits, while difficult, is an important step for you as you move forward and allow God to open your heart. I encourage you to strive to find one good trait. If this is not possible, then perhaps you had a man or woman who chose to mentor you. List traits they had worthy of honoring:

Mother's traits were:

Father's traits were:

Which of these traits do you see in yourself? Are you allowing them to shine?

Dream Walking

Today, as you live your life, note each time you say or do something which honors your earthly parents. If they are living, this may be the ways you choose to interact with them today. If they are deceased, it may be how you honor their memory. As you move through the day, consider how you are honoring your heavenly parent, Abba, or God. Give thanks each time you see the family resemblance between you and God in your words and deeds.

Integrating the Dream

It is essential that you replace thinking that is detrimental to your dreaming with thinking that builds your desire and ability to dream. Notice if you find yourself choosing to think or feel something which stops you from dreaming and walking with God in faith. If you do, place your hand up to your throat as if you were going to choke your-self. Be sure <u>not</u> to apply pressure. This quick physical reminder is a warning to you that this type of thinking chokes the very life and spirit from you. Now move your hand from your throat to your heart. Allow yourself to refill your mind with God's dreams for you. Be sure to refocus your thinking on a portion of a dream or statement of blessing that is important to you. Actively choose life and dreaming.

Consider asking someone close to you to join you in this activity. If either of you becomes aware the conversation is detrimental to dreaming and living life fully, the choking signal is done and followed by moving the hand to the heart. This partnership can help to reveal some thought patterns that may be so familiar to you that you do not initially see them for yourself. It can also add a touch of humor and hope to the process of reshaping your thinking.

Daily Prayer Journal

Date _____   Scripture _____

I rejoice in:

     1.

     2.

     3.

     4.

     5.

I hear God saying to me in the scripture:

Faith and visualization statements I am creating with God:

God and I dream about:

I commit to do the following things with God today:

Day 13

"Why do you see the speck of sawdust in your brother's eye and fail to notice the plank in your own?" Luke 6:41   J.B. Phillips Translation

Reading for the Day: Luke 6:37-42

Dreaming: Who You Talkin' 'Bout?

When I was a teenager, I heard a sermon on this passage that seemed so totally wrong to me. The minister was talking about a psychological phenomenon called "projection." I sat in the balcony and listened to him talk about how what we saw in another person was actually something we projected from ourselves onto them. I truly thought he had been reading way too many books! That would mean that when I thought one of the jocks was arrogant, I was actually the one who was arrogant. It would mean when I thought a teammate was lazy on a school project, it was me who was lazy. It would even mean that when I thought my parents were dull and boring, I was the one who was actually dull and boring. Surely this wasn't true!

At one point in my life, I became very judgmental of people who watched soap operas. What a waste of time! Couldn't they think of something better to do? Here they were caught up in all this fake drama, sometimes for hours on end, when they could be out doing things that would make a difference in the world. Now, I am still not a huge advocate of soap opera watching. However, what was I doing while I was judging them? I was creating a huge drama in my own head! The wasting time, energy and focus that I was judging them for doing, was exactly what I was doing, in just a slightly different form.

It has taken me years to begin to see that today's scripture, "Judge not that you be not judged" is not so much about what God does to us when we judge, but rather about God helping us to understand what is naturally happening to us when we judge. I hate to admit it, but the preacher was right. When we judge, it is because some part of what we are seeing in the other dwells within us. Worse yet, when we are in the midst of judging another, we stop developing, learning and dreaming because we are fixated on the other's need to change and grow. Our options for self-perception and realization are cut off prematurely as we waste our energy focusing on someone who may or may not even be who or what we have projected them to be.

This whole process works for the good as well. If what you see in yourself at any moment is positive, you are much more likely to see the integrity, beauty or creativity in another. I wonder if this is much of what Jesus did. When he spoke to the woman at the well, he knew all that she had done. Still he projected for her the possibility of a different life of real love and grace because that was what was within him. Or what about Peter? How many times did he fail Jesus and himself? Yet, Jesus projected onto him the name of Peter, the very rock on which the church would be built. Jesus was able to dream or imagine who God had created both the woman and Peter to be. No sin within Jesus kept him from seeing what God saw in these two. True, this is not so easy for us, as our sins and biases can much too easily keep us from seeing the dreams God has for us and for others. However, Jesus assumes his disciples will in fact begin to dream beyond their own judgments and dreams. Over and over he demonstrates to them that God is not bound by this world. The leper, the tax collector, the prostitute, the fisherman – many given up on by others - are all seen as treasures to Jesus as he describes God's value of even the least of these in parables.

As you project onto another, it is essential for your growth and the growth of your ability to dream more of God's dreams that you stop and ask yourself what part of you is in the judgment you are placing on them? How are you initiating this judgment and creating the consequences of it for yourself and the other person? What is God dreaming and desiring to project into this person or situation? The words, "the measure you give will be the measure you get," are ones to ponder this day as you seek to dream with God.

Interpreting the Dream

What are some of the most common projections or judgments you make? These may be either critical or positive.

Who or what kinds of people most often are the focus of your judgments?

Select one or two of the critical judgments you most often find yourself making. Prayerfully ask God to demonstrate to you the root within yourself of these judgments. What is God's dream or desire?

Dream Walking

Today as you live your life, notice each time you judge another person. What part of you are you placing on the other person? Lift your judgment up to God and ask God to help you perceive what God sees and desires. Ask God to turn your judgment into a focus that will be life giving for you and the person with whom you are interacting.

Integrating the Dream

It is essential that you replace thinking that is detrimental to your dreaming with thinking that builds your desire and ability to dream. Notice if you find yourself choosing to think or feel something which stops you from dreaming and walking with God in faith. If you do, place your hand up to your throat as if you were going to choke yourself. Be sure <u>not</u> to apply pressure. This quick physical reminder is a warning to you that this type of thinking chokes the very life and spirit from you. Now move your hand from your throat to your heart. Allow yourself to refill your mind with God's dreams for you. Be sure to refocus your thinking on a portion of a dream or statement of blessing that is important to you. Actively choose life and dreaming.

Consider asking someone close to you to join you in this activity. If either of you becomes aware the conversation is detrimental to dreaming and living life fully, the choking signal is done and followed by moving the hand to the heart. This partnership can help to reveal some thought patterns that may be so familiar to you that you do not initially see them for yourself. It can also add a touch of humor and hope to the process of reshaping your thinking.

Daily Prayer Journal

Date _____   Scripture _____

I rejoice in:
      1.
      2.
      3.
      4.
      5.

I hear God saying to me in the scripture:

Faith and visualization statements I am creating with God:

God and I dream about:

I commit to do the following things with God today:

Day 14

"About three hours later it happened that his wife came in not knowing what had taken place. Peter spoke directly to her, 'Tell me, did you sell your land for so much?' 'Yes,' she replied, 'that was it.' Then Peter said to her, 'How could you two have agreed to put the Spirit of the Lord to such a test? Listen, you can hear the footsteps of the men who have just buried your husband coming back through the door, and they will carry you out as well!' Immediately she collapsed at Peter's feet and died." Acts 5:7-10a   J.B. Phillips Translation (I would encourage you to read the entire "Reading for the Day" to get the best understanding of today's passage.)

Reading for the Day: Acts 4:32 - 5:11

Dreaming: Say, "YES!"

A dear friend wanted me to attend a spiritual growth conference. I knew I would just be coming back from a silent retreat and almost a week away from my family. I knew it was not what I really wanted to do, or needed to do, if I were to pursue the dreams God had laid on my heart. Still, she was persistent and persuasive. The conference had made a positive impact on her life and she wanted so much to share it with me. I knew the event would be well planned. It was a good thing. I could certainly grow from going. After much inner debate, I finally said, "Yes, I'll go." My heart, however, was certainly not fully in on the plan. My friend started making arrangements and was very excited about my participation.

While on the silent retreat, God and I did a lot of talking. Every time I thought of leaving so soon on another trip, I came to realize the timing was just not right. There were other things that God wanted me to embrace and engage. God made these clear to me. This was a "good" option; however God had some "great" ones in mind for me to pursue. I kept dancing around this awareness with God. How could I go back on my word? How would my friend ever understand? The more I struggled with this decision, the more I realized that the struggle was not just about this particular commitment. It was about a myriad of things I have said, "yes" to when my heart and dreams clearly required me to say, "no." It was about saying, "I can't," when what I really needed to say was, "I choose not to," or "I won't." Many times, it was not because an option was bad, but rather it was because it was not the best choice God had for me.

I wonder if in today's passage Sapphira was having problems with what to say, "yes" to as well. Had Ananias come up with the idea of selling the land and pretending they gave all the money to the church? Had Sapphira been afraid to stand up to him and refuse to be a part of his lie? Had she tried to convince him to just hold onto the property? Or had she been the one who thought the whole idea up, afraid to tell the other believers they were just not ready to give all of the profits from the sale to the church? No one demanded they sell the land or give all the proceeds to the church. As Peter told Ananias, the land and what to do with the money, had been their decision to make. Sapphira and Ananias had many options they could have whole-heartedly said, "yes" to, but they chose to take the path without integrity. They neither fully gave themselves to their personal concern for resources, nor did they make a full commitment to God and the church in their gift.

It is to Peter's credit that he does not just assume Sapphira knew, or even agreed with, what Ananias had done. He gave her every opportunity to clear herself from this decision. Yet, whether to protect herself or her husband, she chose to lie not only to Peter and the others, but to God as well. The immediate deaths of both Sapphira and Ananias are shocking to say the least. Their physical deaths certainly do catch our attention.

In a much more subtle way, when we repeatedly say, "yes" to things we are not yet ready to say, "yes" to, we experience a form of spiritual numbing or dying that slowly drains us. We do not give ourselves fully to the task. We are frustrated, as is God, that our God-given dreams lay forgotten while we pursue those things which make others happy or us look good. What if Ananias and Sapphira had simply shared their concerns? Perhaps others were struggling as well and a good dialogue could have been started. What if they had prayed and waited until they were excited and joyful about the choice they had made? Perhaps some new ministry effort would need exactly what they had and they would truly want to give the land? What if ...?

You and I are not doing ourselves, others, or God a favor when we take on responsibilities or tasks that detour us away from pursuing our dreams. Our lack of integrity and passion wounds those who really are called to develop the opportunity we are only agreeing to support out of guilt, shame or the desire to be helpful or acknowledged. When we say "yes" to too many things that are not ours to say, "yes" to, our energy is drained, our creativity stifled and our God-given dance left without a dancer.

To what will you say, "YES!" today? May you say it clearly and fulfill God's dreams.

Interpreting

If you were Sapphira, what do you imagine some of your options might have been? What might Peter have said had Sapphira told the truth?

Consider what is on your calendar for the day. How much of it is dream driven? How much of it are you really willing to give 100% of your talents to pursue?

What do you believe the world would be like if each person pursued her/his God-given dream?

Woman at the Jaffa Gate, Jerusalem, Israel
By Holly C. Rudolf

Dream Walking

Notice what you say or do when people ask you to do something today.

If you choose not to do something, are you more likely to say, "I can't," rather than "I won't," or "this is not for me?" Intentionally accept or decline invitations today based on what propels your dreams.

Decide to say "YES!" to one thing today that pursues the dreams of your heart and God's heart.

Are there commitments you have made that need to be renegotiated or finished and not renewed? If so, list the commitment, what needs to change and set a date by which you will complete these adjustments.

Commitment   Adjustment to Be Made   Date to Be Completed

Integrating the Dream

It is essential that you replace thinking that is detrimental to your dreaming with thinking that builds your desire and ability to dream. Notice if you find yourself choosing to think or feel something which stops you from dreaming and walking with God in faith. If you do, place your hand up to your throat as if you were going to choke yourself. Be sure not to apply pressure. This quick physical reminder is a warning to you that this type of thinking chokes the very life and spirit from you. Now move your hand from your throat to your heart. Allow yourself to refill your mind with God's dreams for you. Be sure to refocus your thinking on a portion of a dream or statement of blessing that is important to you. Actively choose life and dreaming.

Consider asking someone close to you to join you in this activity. If either of you becomes aware the conversation is detrimental to dreaming and living life fully, the choking signal is done and followed by moving the hand to the heart. This partnership can help to reveal some thought patterns that may be so familiar to you that you do not initially see them for yourself. It can also add a touch of humor and hope to the process of reshaping your thinking.

Daily Prayer Journal

Date _____   Scripture _____

I rejoice in:

     1.

     2.

     3.

     4.

     5.

I hear God saying to me in the scripture:

Faith and visualization statements I am creating with God:

God and I dream about:

I commit to do the following things with God today:

Day 15

"Create in me a clean heart, O God and put a new and right spirit within me." Psalm 51:10 RSV

Reading for the Day: Psalm 51:1-17

Dreaming: Restoration for Living

It's morning! The alarm goes off, your mind clicks on and what happens next? Visualize your typical morning.

I am generally not a morning person. My seemingly natural response to morning is to sigh and roll over. Does that sound familiar? It was sometime in the midst of my 40's that I was challenged by scripture and some ridiculously cheery risers to realize that how I start and end the day really sets the tone and supports what is in between. Not an easy thing to hear for those of us who do not readily leap out of bed with one of the songs from "The Sound of Music" on our lips. Yet the bookends of rising and moving into rest really are significant for setting the stage for us to dream. As much as I hate to admit it, they are a choice, my choice and your choice.

The scripture today, "Create in me a clean heart, O God, and put a new and right spirit within me." (Psalm 51:10 RSV) is a prayerful request and petition to God for help and renewal. In the midst of fear of enemies and the shadows of sin, the writer makes this passionate plea, fully expecting that God will create in him something new and beautiful. It is clearly not a passive request. The psalmist is asking God to cleanse him from the inside out and open him to teach (vs. 13), to sing of God's deliverance (vs. 14) and to praise (vs.15). He wants to be an active part of the transformation, rather than expecting God to magically do it all for him.

When I am in those early waking moments, it seems so innocent to whine about the cold or the darkness or the long day I have ahead. Yet those thoughts steal precious moments from me that can direct me to God and God's opportunities for me that day. By choosing what is holy and good, and, yes, joyful and sometimes humorous, I free my heart to be cleansed by joy and to allow the power of God's spirit to build in me with each breath. I can experience restoration of my joy in God. My spirit can be renewed and set right. I can begin dream walking and anticipating a day of partnership with God as I seek to be a vital part of what God is doing.

Because of the incredible importance of those early morning minutes, I have made it a prayer discipline to catch myself as soon as I can when I wake and smile. I then intentionally laugh. Generally speaking, my laugh is not hearty in the early hours of the morning. Yet that smile and laughter begins a cycle of joy within me that truly is cleansing, both spiritually and physically. God has made our bodies in such an amazing way that smiling and laughter create endorphins that help with healing, inspiration and can even curb depression. Endorphins build our immune systems and are God's gift to us for cleansing and empowering our physical bodies. It even takes fewer muscles to smile than to frown – an important point for those of us who struggle with the discipline of exercising regularly! Smiling and laughing are like opening a gift from God each morning as I first awake.

I have always felt the end of the day when I slide into bed and snuggle under the covers is much like returning to the womb of God. The support of the bed, the quietness of the night, the settling of my breathing, are all joyful blessings after a full day. I take a few minutes to review the day. In what ways did I really participate fully in God's dreams today? Where did I miss the mark? What are the hopes and dreams God has for me in the days ahead? Last of all I give thanks and feel the joy in me once again restored as I recognize God's presence in me and around me. I then finish the day with a smile and God's goodnight hug.

I encourage you to intentionally create rituals for rising up and going to sleep that you repeat as naturally as getting out of bed. Find ones that truly help to restore your joy and connection to God. Make them ones you look forward to in those waking and entering into rest moments. If you already have a ritual, is it supporting your growth? Is it a meaningless habit or a ritual that creates a sense of God's presence with you? Make a choice to begin and end the day with passion and joy.

Interpreting the Dream

What do you currently do when you first wake up in the morning? What types of feelings/thoughts do you experience as you do this?

What do you currently do when you go to sleep? What types of feelings/thoughts do you experience as you do this?

If you are not currently experiencing joy and renewal on waking or when going to sleep, what types of activity would help you to experience this first thing in the morning and the last thing of the day? Some ideas include smiling, laughing, touching someone you love, playing inspirational music, reciting scripture, singing a song, doing a breathing prayer or meditation, dancing, stretching, or showering. What others can you think of that are helpful to you?

Dream Walking

Interview someone today who is successful. Successful in this case is defined by you in whatever way you define it. Ask her/him what they do or experience as they awake and as they go to sleep. How does God fit into their rituals?

If possible, watch a small child awake or fall asleep. What do you notice her or him doing? For those who can not actually watch a child, remember what you have noticed in children in the past. Is there anything you observe that would be helpful to include in your own rising and falling asleep?

At night and in the morning for the next few weeks, practice intentionally going to sleep and waking in the way you consciously choose to help you experience God and life more fully. You may want to put a reminder on or near your alarm clock or a poster on the wall to help you remember you are changing something today. Notice how you experience life in the in-between times. Do you notice any difference? Ask someone near you to be an accountability partner as you intentionally change your habits.

Integrating the Dream

Take time to breathe in slowly through your nose and out through your mouth. Then smile. Repeat this three times. At the end of the cycle, joyfully appreciate being a daughter of God.

Daily Prayer Journal

Date _____   Scripture _____

I rejoice in:
     1.
     2.
     3.
     4.
     5.

I hear God saying to me in the scripture:

Faith and visualization statements I am creating with God:

God and I dream about: (After writing dreams for today, look back over the last two weeks of dreams. How are they similar or different? Have you made any actions towards making these dreams realities?)

I commit to do the following things with God today:

Day 16

"But let all who take refuge in you rejoice; let them ever sing for joy. Spread your protection over them, so that those who love your name may exult in you. For you bless the righteous, O LORD; you cover them with favour as with a shield." Psalm 5:11-12 NRSV

Reading for the Day: Psalm 5:1-12

Dreaming: Give Me Refuge, Oh God!

What is it that you have given power to create anxiety in you? Is it your children? Your spending habits? Your job? Your friendships? Heavy traffic? Your extended family? It is important to recognize whatever it is you give the power to create a shadow over your countenance or fear in your heart. You are the one making this choice. A child missing curfew, a dissatisfied employer or an angry spouse are all events. You are the one who decides whether to be upset and anxious, optimistic and hopeful, or perhaps neutral.

This is very hard to believe. Wouldn't anyone be upset if their child was drinking and driving? Wouldn't anyone lose heart if betrayed by a friend? Yet think of some of the great leaders you admire. People like Jesus, Ghandi, Eleanor Roosevelt, Dr. Martin Luther King, Jr., Maya Angelou, Oprah Winfrey, etc. We recognize they chose not to be defined by events in their lives. Each one chose to be more than the events around them. They give us the example that we, too, can see amazing possibilities in every event.

When we repeat phrases like, "I am depressed," or "I am anxious," or "I am weary and frustrated," we give more power to these feelings. If we really want God's joy, we can acknowledge our fears and concerns and then clearly choose joy.

As the youngest of four children, when I felt left out of the family discussions, I would typically go and hide in the walk-in closet upstairs. Sometimes I would be missed and other times no one noticed I had disappeared. I always felt safe among the clothes and other items in that closet. It became my castle and my refuge. My feelings of frustration and loneliness usually transformed as I began to use my mind and energy to create an amazing world. I sometimes fell asleep and woke up renewed and ready to reenter the family network.

When you are feeling anxious, fearful or alone, one option is to do as the psalmist did—take refuge in God and rejoice. The rejoicing may not come immediately. As you take refuge in God in your mind, you can say to God, "I am opening myself to your strength and your power." Your focus, your faith, your energy and visualization then become connected to God and not on multiplying whatever concern is plaguing you. You choose to dream walk with God rather than to live in a nightmare you are helping to create and sustain.

What thoughts will you ponder today? What song will you sing? What dream will you dare to dream?

Interpreting the Dream

Is there currently a thought or emotion that burdens you? If so, define it clearly in one or two words. Spend a minimum of 5 minutes sitting with your arms and hands open in a position of receiving. Repeat, "I am releasing _____ and opening myself to Your strength and Your power," out loud ten times and then listen. Feel God's presence within and around you. What are the possibilities God has in mind for you and for the world? If your mind begins to dwell on any thought or emotion that is binding your joy and ability to dream during the day, repeat this exercise, preferably out loud. Always listen, as it is in the listening and receiving that you will begin to find a new path to healing and strength.

If you are not currently feeling burdened – Praise God! Repeat only "I am opening myself to Your strength and Your power," to further increase your creativity, focus and dreaming.

Stairway at Tel Meggido, Israel
By Holly C. Rudolf

Dream Walking

(See Appendix A for clarification of visualization, if needed.) Go to your sacred place for visualization. After you have centered or focused yourself there, start walking until you find a cave, or a house, or perhaps even a womb that God has created for you. Use whatever image works best for you. Enter into this refuge God has for you. Notice what is in that space. What do you feel or hear? Notice there is safety with God. Experience God's attention and renewing presence. Ask God for guidance and listen. See with God the deepest desires of your heart. When you are ready, take from this place the hope and passion you need to live out the dreams God has placed in you.

Integrating the Dream

Take time to breathe in slowly through your nose and out through your mouth. Then smile. Repeat this three times. At the end of the cycle, joyfully appreciate being a daughter of God.

Daily Prayer Journal

Date _____   Scripture _____

I rejoice in:
      1.
      2.
      3.
      4.
      5.

I hear God saying to me in the scripture:

Faith and visualization statements I am creating with God:

God and I dream about:

I commit to do the following things with God today:

Day 17

"We will not hide them from their children; we will tell to the coming generation the glorious deeds of the LORD, and his might, and the wonders that he has done." Psalm 78:4 NRSV

Reading for the Day: Psalm 78:1-72

Dreaming: I Love to Tell the Story

My mother was an artful storyteller. At any family gathering, she could be found retelling the stories of her father's homesteading, early married life with Dad, and stories about each of our births and shenanigans. One of my favorites was of her teaching in a two-room school house out in western Kansas. Some men had been breaking into classrooms at surrounding schools and taking what they could, but she hadn't thought much about it. She had stayed late in the afternoon to work on papers and heard some men breaking into the other classroom. She slipped out a window as quietly as she could, praying as she went for her movement to be unheard and unseen by the men in the other room. My mother, all of 19, 5' 5" and 90 pounds, sprinted across the fields to the home where she was staying. She called the sheriff who managed to get there just in time to arrest the two men. It always made me feel like my mom and her God were invincible each time she told the story.

The stories my mother told us most generally had happy endings, at least the ones she told us when we were young. The stories encouraged us to seek God, to believe in miracles, to be brave, to use all of our wits and, yes, many of her stories were funny. It wasn't until I was older that I heard the other stories - ones about her having polio, almost dying from a burst appendix, fearing she would never walk after a spinal fusion, losing babies before they were full term and even losing her first fiancé at Pearl Harbor.

I realize now that the stories my mother told were ones that have served me well in life. Her choice to fill my mind with adventure and possibilities was a gift for which I can never repay her. The times she made me the "special one" in the story built my self esteem. The times when someone messed up and managed to find their way again encouraged me when I made mistakes. She had an easy way of weaving God into the stories. Her stories were told as though everyone surely could see the thread of God's presence in the midst of the characters and their experiences.

In Psalm 78, the writer makes it clear that we must tell the children of the world the "glorious deeds of the Lord." It is our responsibility and honor to share the wonders which God has done. The Psalmist chooses to focus on the Exodus of the people from Egypt. Over and over the people would be amazed by God's power and guidance and then seemingly suddenly refuse to follow God's commandments. Again the people would find themselves in closer relationship to God and yet again, they would slip away. This fickleness is somewhat hard for us to believe as we look back on their experiences. How could they have doubted God's continued faithfulness and love for them? However, how often do we find ourselves clearly standing with God and treasuring our relationship and then slowly, yet all too surely, find that we have slipped away and focused on other things that are far less important?

By knowing the story of the people in Exodus, we hear our own story. What attracts us? What stories do we wish would have a different ending? By hearing their stories, we can make a choice in our own lives to write a similar ending or to come up with a whole new scenario. We can be inspired by these and many other stories to grow into greater awareness and abundance in our relationship with God.

For some of us, sharing the stories of our faith does not come easily. We are perhaps shy or uncertain how others will experience our dreams and experiences with God. Yet it is essential that we share our stories of faith and dreams so that we and others may hear and respond and grow. Our story may be the very thing that ignites in another a new dream, a new passion, a new depth of love for God. Their response may also bring us to greater understanding of God's activities in the story. In telling our story, we also hear anew the power of God's presence in our own lives. Speak the stories God has placed in your heart. Speak them boldly and clearly to those who desire to hear. May we each truly love to tell the story of God, that all people might know and remember the One in Whom we live and move and have our being.

Interpreting the Dream

Our stories make us unique. They are the special way God has touched our lives by keeping us safe, creating miracles with us, healing us and guiding us to abundant life. What stories have touched you? These could be stories from the Bible, literature, or personal experiences. Are there stories you have been afraid to share? If so, what frightens you? Do you believe others could be blessed by you sharing these stories? Think of these stories of faith and list 10.

    1.
    2.
    3.
    4.
    5.
    6.
    7.
    8.
    9.
    10.

Select one of these stories. Think for a minute about the details of the story. Jot them down. What makes this story powerful for you?

Dream Walking

Name 3 people who could benefit from hearing this story from you.
    1.
    2.
    3.

Go to visit or call at least one of the three people listed above. Share the story and see what story they have to share.

Read or sing the hymn, "I Love to Tell the Story," by Katherine Hankey and William G. Fischer. How do these words touch you?

Integrating the Dream

Take time to breathe in slowly through your nose and out through your mouth. Then smile. Repeat this three times. At the end of the cycle, joyfully appreciate being a daughter of God.

Daily Prayer Journal

Date _____   Scripture _____

I rejoice in:
    1.
    2.
    3.
    4.
    5.

I hear god saying to me in the scripture:

Faith and visualization statements I am creating with God:

God and I dream about:

I commit to do the following things with God today:

Day 18

"Jesus wept." John 11:35 RSV

Reading for the Day: John 11:1-57

Dreaming: Good Grief

Grief is a strange thing. Sometimes it is so obvious, clear and apparent to me. I know what I am grieving about. I can feel and sense the memory or loss that is touching my heart. Then there are the days when I am talking about something totally different and tears rise up in my eyes. I am not even sure how or what started it until I stop, breathe and become aware of the loss I need to honor, feel and release.

When Jesus heard Lazarus was ill, he waited. There were many who thought he should not go at all. It was too dangerous. He had been run out of the area before and hostilities with those in power were rising. Others wondered why he delayed when he loved Lazarus, Mary and Martha so much. At the right time, Jesus went. He knew God's power would be revealed as God's love was made visible through the miraculous raising of Lazarus from the dead.

The shortest verse in most English translations of the Bible, certainly everyone's favorite for the purpose of memorization, will remain, in part, a mystery. Jesus knew he would raise Lazarus from the dead. So it isn't likely he was crying for Lazarus. Was he crying because Mary and Martha were so hurt and unable to see God creating something far greater than only healing Lazarus? Or was he just weary of people assuming the worst in him when he wanted them to see in him and in themselves the best, the kingdom of God dwelling within them? This will be a good question for Jesus one day. However, what is clear is that, what-ever was bringing Jesus grief, he took time to allow himself to weep, to feel and to honor what was touching his heart. Only then did he heal Lazarus.

There is no time line for grieving. It can last for a few minutes or for years. When we really allow ourselves to weep, to recognize what we are missing that we so deeply cherished and to understand what is no longer, we honor our grief. We eventually come to a point where we can again decide to choose to live life fully.

In the mini-series, "True Women," a pioneer woman lost her husband. He was a Texas Ranger who fought in several conflicts. He died falling off a horse coming home – not at all what she had feared. She went into deep grieving. She wanted only to be left alone as she sat clothed in black. Every day was a repetition of the day before - she would sob until she could not sob and then enter into a kind of numbness until she could sob again. About three months later, she received a letter from her younger sister and it jarred her back into life. She walked to her husband's grave and started a fire. She talked to him and released him, promising to carry the memory of his love with her as she lived her life fully. She burned her black widow's dress and a smile from deep within her rose up on her tear stained cheeks. It was time to move through her grief.

There is great wisdom in acknowledging and naming our grief. Hiding from grief, most generally increases it and creates a kind of numbness that pulls us away from living life fully with God. Each of us will experience it in unique ways. Tears, anger, denial, fear and acceptance are just some of the stages of grieving. For some, the journey of grief is best done alone. Others desire companions on the journey. Listening to God's guidance through prayerful searching will direct our steps. The same God who made us human also gave us the ability to receive, let go, grieve and be renewed. God is faithful to walk with us through the process of grieving if we will open ourselves to God's presence.

Interpreting the Dream

What has been a time or source of grief for you that you have moved through successfully? What did you do that helped you to move through your grief?

Are you currently dealing with any issues of grief?

If so, try writing a letter to the person or about the situation freely, saying the words on your heart. Give this exercise the best of your energy and honesty. When you are finished, the letter is yours to do with as you choose. What is important is the cleansing this can create. Even as tears create endorphins in the body which uplift and heal, so, too, can writing down emotions help to cleanse the heart.

Dream Walking

Today consider creating or buying some type of food that has significance to your family history. What makes this food special? Who made it? Who ate it? Choose a friend, or someone who is perhaps grieving themselves, to share this dish with either today or on a day you schedule in the coming week.

Watch the children's movie, "Land Before Time," with a friend or on your own this week. What does Little Foot learn about grief as he finds his way through the loss of his mother?

For those wanting additional help with grief, I highly recommend, <u>Good Grief,</u> by Granger Westberg. It is an inexpensive, short, easy to read, highly practical book.

Integrating the Dream

Take time to breathe in slowly through your nose and out through your mouth. Then smile. Repeat this three times. At the end of the cycle, joyfully appreciate being a daughter of God.

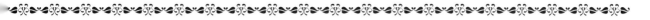

Daily Prayer Journal

Date _____   Scripture _____

I rejoice in:

    1.

    2.

    3.

    4.

    5.

I hear God saying to me in the scripture:

Faith and visualization statements I am creating with God:

God and I dream about:

I commit to do the following things with God today:

Girls' Basketball Team at Missouri Western University
By Holly C. Rudolf

Day 19

"Or do you not know that your body is a temple of the Holy Spirit within you, which you have from God, and that you are not your own? For you were bought with a price; therefore glorify God in your body." I Corinthians 6:19-20   NRSV

Reading for the Day: I Corinthians 6:12-20

Dreaming: Keeping the Temple for Dream Walking

Close your eyes for a minute and imagine what you look like. Notice the color and tone of your skin and your hair. What is the shape of your body? What do your eyes look like? Are you smiling, straight faced or frowning?

Now take a peek in the mirror. What do you see? Is what you see similar to what you imagined at first? Do you see a body that is well fed, well exercised and well rested? Do you see someone who has cherished the gift of their physical body or someone who has occasionally taken it for granted? If your body were taken to a used body dealer, what kind of trade-in value would you get?

When I read this verse, I find myself wanting to hide. Eating foods like pizza, ice cream, donuts, etc. is a real temptation for me. The thought of exercise for most of my life has been something relegated to P.E. classes and I usually signed up for as few of those as possible. It always seemed there was too much to do in any given day without worrying about exercise, too. I was fortunate. I ate pretty much what I wanted to and got away with it as long as my metabolism was high. Then the 40's hit. Something happened to the body God had given me and it wasn't pretty. My energy was slowing down, excess weight was creeping in, and the allergies I'd had since I was a teenager were ever present.

About that time I began researching, looking for alternatives to help with our son's asthma, allergies and mild ADD.   I was surprised at how many experts recommended nutritionals. And they weren't the ones making money from specific products. There was a lot of information about fighting free radicals in the body and discussion about soil depletion and the reduction of nutrients in our foods. Now you have to understand that, with the exception of during pregnancy, vitamins were something I saw as only for the easily snookered folks. "If you can't get it in regular food, who needs it?" I thought.

The more I read, the more convinced I was that our son needed nutritional supplements. My husband and I discussed it and decided that not only would we purchase nutritionals for Nate, but we would also start taking a daily regimen ourselves to support and encourage him. Now mind you, I did not expect anything to happen for us, but I hoped something would happen for Nate. (How many times have I refused to change something for myself, but finally made the change for my children or others I love? Does that sound familiar to you?)

Next problem—which nutritional? In the store there were so many options it made my head spin. One company said they were the best available in any market, another claimed they had superior "natural" elements. Still another marketed itself to be the latest in nutritional science. Some said they were water soluble. Others said they had fast absorption. Where was a novice like me to get the information needed to buy the right product?

With some reading and help from friends, I settled on one line of pharmaceutical grade nutritional products. Long story short, in spite of my negative attitude, we saw results. Allergy medication was set aside. Asthma medication was used less and less frequently until we had inhalants expiring before they were empty. Bill was able to stop taking a medication to handle the effects of his Restless Leg Syndrome. My administrative assistant commented quite innocently, "You know your dark circles are gone and you're easier to get along with." – Yes, she is still working with me! She became so intrigued that she tried the nutritionals for her Fibromyalgia, something that had plagued her for years. She was amazed that she slept well for the first time in a long time in just a few days after starting the products. Over time her pain and swelling was greatly reduced! The quality of her life was changed drastically.

I found that the better I felt and the more energy I had, the easier it was to be open and ready to spend more time dream walking with God. Instead of using most of my energy to do the simple functions of life, I could focus more on the people around me. Fewer colds and sicknesses added to the number of days each year I could give 100% to living life.

Though God can clearly use illness and pain to help us grow closer to God, I do not believe God causes us to be ill or desires for us to be so. I know the reduction of medications with side effects and my cells regenerating with increasing strength has made a huge difference in my life. For me and most of us, health, or the lack of it, will be a lifelong choice.

God has given us the gift of our physical bodies. I'm certain God has often wondered why I wasn't more careful with that gift. Why would any of us metaphorically leave our bodies outside to rust by what we eat and our inactivity?

As you complete "Interpreting," I strongly encourage you to consider your body as it is today and how you desire it to be to best dream walk with God. What can you realistically change that will make a difference? I wish you well on your journey towards greater health. I look forward to hearing of your successes. Health is truly a continuum, one which we can shift each day with prayer and care.

Interpreting

Take a look in a full length mirror. What about your body is exactly as it needs to be for you to have energy and strength each day? What is detouring you from greater health?

On a scale of 1 to 10, 1 being "I don't have any" and 10 being "I have more than enough," answer the following questions. Circle your answer.

I eat at least 3 servings of fruits and vegetables each day.

| 1 | 2 | 3 | 4 | 5 | 6 | 7 | 8 | 9 | 10 |

I exercise 30 minutes a day, 4 times per week.

| 1 | 2 | 3 | 4 | 5 | 6 | 7 | 8 | 9 | 10 |

I sleep well each night.

| 1 | 2 | 3 | 4 | 5 | 6 | 7 | 8 | 9 | 10 |

I get enough sleep each night.

| 1 | 2 | 3 | 4 | 5 | 6 | 7 | 8 | 9 | 10 |

My energy level is great!

| 1 | 2 | 3 | 4 | 5 | 6 | 7 | 8 | 9 | 10 |

My perfect weight is _____. I need to stay the same, add or decrease by _____pounds.

Go to your place of renewal in meditation/visualization. Sit there as you are today. Imagine a large screen in front of you. Picture yourself 5 years from now in greater health than you are today. What activities are you enjoying? How do you look? Advance the movie to 10 years from today. Again, what do you see yourself doing? What type of exercise do you enjoy? Imagine yourself feeling truly well with no medications. Continue this exercise to the age to which you desire to live. Picture yourself in great health at each stage feeling strong and capable. Return to the present and give thanks for where you are today. What, if any, commitments do you desire to cause your visualizations of health and wellness to become a reality?

Dream Walking

Exercise is essential. At a minimum, commit to a 15 minute walk, dancing to a song in your living room or doing stretches today. Many of you may be exceeding this already and that is wonderful! If so, be sure to celebrate your choice to exercise today. Ideally, each of us would do aerobic exercise for a minimum of 30 minutes, with 5 minutes to warm up and cool down, three or four times a week. Is this something you want in your life? What is your commitment? Share your commitment with someone you love and perhaps partner with a friend to exercise together if this encourages you to keep your commitment to yourself.

Integrating the Dream

Take time to breathe in slowly through your nose and out through your mouth. Then smile. Repeat this three times. At the end of the cycle, joyfully appreciate being a daughter of God.

Daily Prayer Journal

Date _____   Scripture _____

I rejoice in:
1.
2.
3.
4.
5.

I hear God saying to me in the scripture:

Faith and visualization statements I am creating with God:

God and I dream about:

I commit to do the following things with God today:

Day 20

"Saul the son of Kish was taken by lot. But when they sought him, he could not be found. So they inquired again of the LORD, 'Did the man come here?' and the LORD said, 'See, he has hidden himself among the baggage.'" 1 Samuel 10:21 b & 22 NRSV

Reading for the Day: 1 Samuel 10:1 – 11:15

Dreaming: Coming Out of the Baggage

Have you ever had the sense that you were to step out and take action? Have you ever known you were the one with the solution? Perhaps you jumped right in and made things happen. Or maybe you allowed yourself to hide behind modesty or shyness as those who were more verbal led the way, possibly not even in the best direction.

If you have ever stepped back and away from a dream, then you have something in common with King Saul and the majority of the human race. Saul was tall and handsome and apparently had leadership skills. Yet when the prophet Samuel proclaimed he would be king, Saul was mystified, perhaps even afraid. Samuel did not speak to Saul for God with a still small voice. Rather, Samuel anointed Saul with oil clearly proclaiming God's mission for him (vs. 1).   Saul then experienced confirmation of that anointing by other prophets singing and dancing (vs. 5) and finally by the drawing of lots (vs. 21). Still when it came time to step up and claim his purpose, Saul hid. He hid behind a bunch of baggage. How odd it must have been to have the people run and fetch their new king from his hiding place. How frightening and yet inspiring it must have been for Saul to hear the people proclaim, "Long live the king!" (vs. 24) as they brought him before Samuel.

Saul had a purpose. What if you have been given a purpose to carry out in your life? What if who you have been created to be, the experiences you have had since birth and even your passions and desires come together to uniquely form you to bring a gift to the world and to yourself? What if in one lifetime you will do many great things, yet your heart will not rest until you claim and accept your purpose?

Sometime after I turned 40, I began to search for the purpose God had for me in the unfolding of God's dreams. Yet I struggled to really name my purpose. I had lots of great things that I did: I was a mom, a wife, a retreat leader, a preacher. Yet, for me, that set of identities was not clear enough to provide direction and focus in times of ease and distress. Through prayer, visualization, workshops with Klemmer and Associates (www.klemmer.com) and continuing to look at my gifts, I slowly began to peel away the many things to the one thing that connected all the things I do with passion. This is my overarching commitment to God, to myself, and to all those I meet:

> *My purpose is to enter fully into the joy of God and rekindle the*
> *power and beauty of that joy in myself and others.*

As I step further and further into that purpose, so many things are more vivid and clear. For one, writing this book and helping women to find and re-find the joy of God in their lives has become a high priority. For another, I have made time in my schedule to facilitate more retreats to help people experience life changing activities that can carry new alternatives and choices into their daily lives. When I enter into a group where I know few, if any, my first inclination to hide behind my shyness can be set aside as I seek ways to truly bring joy into the conversations and activities. What a relief it is not to hide because I am unsure of what God has uniquely called me to be.

From the time we are born, we start collecting the baggage we hide behind. For some of us it is anger, sadness, fear or disillusionment. For others, the baggage may be low self esteem, control or the desire to be perfect. When we find our true purpose, the need for this baggage can be released. When we step fully into who we are created to be and live out our purpose, we become magnets for opportunities and for people who either need what we can share or who can partner with us in our joint purposes.

Saul in 1 Samuel 11 first picks up his mantel as king when the people of Jabesh are under siege. He is not afraid to demand the allegiance of all the people to save the town of Jabesh. Because Saul claimed his authority and his purpose, the people of Jabesh were rescued. What would have happened if Saul had continued to hide? Who would have stepped forward? During this time in Israel's history, Saul and the people were greatly blessed. Sadly, Saul later forgot his purpose. (1 Samuel 15) He not only lost God's favor; he also lost the joy he had in leading the people. He became ineffective, paranoid and dangerous to those he had been called to lead and serve.

What is your purpose? Are you living it each moment of every day? Do you know your purpose so well that it helps you to be grounded in times of great joy, high stress or confusion? If your purpose is not yet clear, I encourage you to pursue the "Interpreting the Dream" exercises. Follow up with them daily until you have claimed a clear and compelling purpose. God has created all of us to be dream walkers with God. Find your purpose and you will find your passion, your energy, your guide to dreaming intentionally with God.

Interpreting the Dream

Without giving thought or judgment to your responses, write as many endings to the following as you can in 5 minutes.

My purpose in life is to:

Call three people who know you well and ask them to tell you three things they see you involved with or doing where they experience you as giving 100%.

Write a eulogy for yourself as you desire it to be written by someone you love and respect. This is not just about who you have been. It is also about who you desire to be in the time you have left on this planet.

Using the meditation and visualization techniques as described in Appendix A, see yourself in your place of comfort and renewal. Allow yourself to sit in this place of renewal fully seeing what is around you, hearing the sounds, smelling the aromas, touching the surfaces around you and fully entering into the experience. At a distance, God is approaching you. God has many forms, so allow yourself to be aware of how God comes to you. God reaches out to you or envelops you. You talk together. God says to you, "I have made you for this time and this place. I have made you for _____."

Dwell in this time with God. Embrace the love and power God has for you. You are God's beloved and God desires for you to be whole and complete. When you have shared your heart with God, God will slowly and gently leave you as a physical form. You remain confident God's spirit is always present in and around you. Claim the words God has given to you. When you are ready, open your eyes and return to awareness of your surroundings.

Look again at the phrases you wrote in the first exercise. Using what God shared with you in the visualization and the other exercises, is there a phrase or sentence that you are drawn to? If not, I encourage you to make one up based on what you now know and live with it for a time until you find the one that fully awakens your soul. You and your purpose are unique and greatly needed as God moves among us on the earth.

Dream Walking

Write your purpose on a piece of paper and place it on your mirror. Each morning and evening, repeat this phrase a minimum of three times. Include this in your daily time of prayer. Listen for God's response to you as you claim your purpose. If you are musical, consider creating a melody to sing. If you enjoy dancing and movement, create movements that embed the words into your physical memory as well. It is important to begin this practice. Do not worry at first about "getting it right." Be open to the unfolding of your purpose as you step into what you know right now.

Integrating the Dream

Take time to breathe in slowly through your nose and out through your mouth. Then smile. Repeat this three times. At the end of the cycle, joyfully appreciate being a daughter of God.

Daily Prayer Journal

Date _____   Scripture _____

I rejoice in:
      1.
      2.
      3.
      4.
      5.

I hear God saying to me in the scripture:

Faith and visualization statements I am creating with God:

God and I dream about:

I commit to do the following things with God today:

Day 21

"Then he said to them, 'Go your way, eat the fat and drink sweet wine and send portions of them to those for whom nothing is prepared, for this day is holy to our Lord; and do not be grieved, for the joy of the Lord is your strength.'" Nehemiah 8:10 NRSV

Reading for the Day: Nehemiah 7:73 - 8:12

Dreaming: The Joy of the Lord Is Your Strength

The people in today's passage had lost touch with the impact and truth of God's presence in the scriptures. At first little pieces were lost, and over time God's Word became hidden to them. When Ezra brought the Law of Moses to all the people, unusually so to both men and women, it was as though some of them understood for the first time just how hidden they were from the power of God's presence within them. How could they not have known? How could they have been so disobedient?

Their first response was to weep. How many times had they failed God? How many times had they ached and suffered when all they had to do was step out in faith and seek God? What a loss they felt. How much fuller life would have been with God and God's ways in their lives.

Sometimes I am like these people; perhaps you are as well. I know God is here. I talk to God daily. I believe in God's power and partnership with me, yet I do not always open myself up to the fullness of God's presence. I'm not sure why I do this, but I know I do. It is as though I cycle into the depths of God and then something in me pulls away, not yet certain if I am willing or able to surrender to God and claim my calling.

When my husband and I were pastoring separate churches, each of us came home one evening worn out and weary. In both congregations there were individuals and issues that we were struggling to understand. It seemed that the harder we worked and did all the things we knew how to do, including praying, the less the situations improved. I don't remember why, but somehow we started talking about laying on hands in prayer to encourage and empower people. It hit us both at almost the same time that the only times we had laid hands on one another was during each of our ordination services. Why did we not use this gift of prayer and empowerment that God so freely gives to encourage each other?

That night we laid hands on one another as we prayed. I won't tell you everything magically flipped. I will tell you that each of us gained a sense of peace and strength. Like the people of Israel, I also had a sense of sorrow and guilt that here I was a pastor and long time Christian and I was hiding from some of the tools God freely gave to me. Fortunately, I chose not to stay long in this grief. For that, too, is a form of denying God's power and presence. I realized that I could mourn what I had missed or that I could instead celebrate the incredible gold mine I had found and choose to stand in God's power more fully. Choosing to stand in God's joy and power is a daily choice and spiritual discipline for all of us.

With the guidance of Nehemiah and Ezra, the people in today's passage also chose not to stubbornly cling to their grief and sorrow at their failure to fully live in the Word of God. They rose up as a people and each went out to honor and celebrate God's Word by claiming the joy and power it brings. They accepted the joy of worshipping and serving God. Through stepping into their joy, they found strength to accept the past and to move into the future with hope and confidence. To sing, to dance, to feast and, yes, to celebrate finding God anew is a far greater life plan than to beat oneself – physically or metaphorically. God's forgiveness and grace are always available. Like a loving parent, God is not so much concerned about where we have been than as about where we are choosing to go.

How wise small children are. Think of how they learn to walk. When they fall they rarely waste more than a few moments on tears or anger. They get up and try again. And oh, how much energy and enthusiasm they put into their efforts. Watching a little one take that first step and seeing the pride and joy in her/his face is a gift each time I see it. Children are wise. Little time is spent mourning the past. They most often move quickly into what brings them joy.

Some of the people with greatest joy in God are those who recognize how completely lost they were before they discovered God in their lives. There is no confusion for them about God's power to heal, uplift and guide. They have moved from shame and guilt to renewal and hope and the abundance of joy they experience in that movement is life transforming.

Think on how "the joy of the Lord is your strength" today. Dare to celebrate God's presence around you, within you and within those you meet. Dare to dream God will do great things through you and others today.

Mother and Daughter Having Fun
By Josef B. Rudolf

Interpreting the Dream

At what level do you most generally experience God's joy within you? On a scale of 1 -10, 1 being not at all and 10 being always, rate your experience.

1   2   3   4   5   6   7   8   9   10

When you dream walk with God, what do you feel?

Think of a time when you had lost a sense of God's guiding hand and presence. What were you doing? How did you recognize you were missing the power of God's Word in your life?

As you read today's scripture, did you come to any new understandings of God's Word to you? Spend a few moments pondering the phrase "the joy of the Lord." What does that mean to you? What do you imagine it means to God?

Dream Walking

The Jewish people, as well as people of most religions and cultures, have cyclical celebrations that remind people of their story and faith. What do you and your family do to celebrate the presence of God in your life?

Do you have any daily ways of celebrating?

If not, would you like to add one or more? Talk about this with your family and dream about options together. Some alternatives might include a unique hug or greeting, a special plate or glass for celebrating birthdays or events, sharing experiences with God at a meal, cooking together, singing together, bedtime stories, dancing together, head rubs, prayer together, creating artistic works together, dreaming together daily, taking a trip to a place where God has been doing or completed a unique work, etc.

Integrating the Dream

Take time to breathe in slowly through your nose and out through your mouth. Then smile. Repeat this three times. At the end of the cycle, joyfully appreciate being a daughter of God.

Daily Prayer Journal

Date _____   Scripture _____

I rejoice in:
1.
2.
3.
4.
5.

I hear God saying to me in the scripture:

Faith and visualization statements I am creating with God:

God and I dream about:

I commit to do the following things with God today:

Day 22

"When she and her household had been baptized she appealed to us, saying, 'If you are satisfied that I am a true believer in the Lord, then come down to my house and stay there.'"
Acts 16:15   J.B. Phillips Translation

Reading for the Day: Acts 16:11-40

Dreaming: Stepping Out

Go back in time and imagine for a moment your name is Lydia. You are a truly unique woman living in the first century A.D. Women in your time are legally considered to be the property of a man. You have no man in your life who owns you. This is a rare gift. On the other hand, in a legal system that denies your legitimacy, there is no man to step up and handle legal issues for you. It has not been an easy journey for you as you have become an incredibly successful business woman and the head of your own household.

When you first started your business, people laughed at your dream. How could a woman run a business? Everyone knew that was a man's job. Yet your skill with making and using the coveted purple dyes had slowly built an elite, wealthy and powerful clientele. Because you had what they wanted, they tolerated you being a woman. Some even found it interesting.

You have many servants and slaves who help with the tedious task of making the purple dye. You may have some sisters, children or grandchildren of your own still living with you. There is never a need for you to carry water or do the menial tasks around the house, yet sometimes you choose to go down to the riverside where the women gather water and wash the clothes. For the most part, you enjoy their company and the conversation. It isn't always easy being a woman with the freedom to choose her own path when others have so few options. Many resent you for being different. Others hope secretly, and some not so secretly, to be like you. Though some do not trust you, they still include you in conversations.

Today the riverside is abuzz with conversation. The women are talking with three male strangers. As you listen, you realize they are followers of Jesus. How freely Paul, Silas and Timothy speak with the women. You are amazed! You have heard that these strange followers of Jesus treat men and women alike – all as beloved children of God – but you can hardly believe what you are seeing! You want to hear every word they have to say. You listen with a mind trained through years of working with cloth to look for inconsistencies and flaws. Could this Jesus be whom they say? You dare to ask one question and then another. This Jesus is truly the one for whom you have been looking. With all of your heart and soul you know that this is the truth you have longed for and you accept Christ and are baptized. Not only you, but your entire household, are baptized and enter into new life in Christ.

Filled with joy and gratitude, you realize the travelers must need a place to stay. Without fear, speaking against custom and social status, you say to the preachers, "If you have judged me to be faithful to the Lord, come to my house and stay." Do you hear a gasp or two when you make this invitation? What do you see on the faces of Paul, Silas and Timothy? You insist they come and stay and they accept!

What kinds of things do you learn from them? What do you hope to find in this new relationship with Christ? What talents do you bring to the family of God?

I have often wondered if Lydia, along with Priscilla, were part of Paul's inspiration to write Galatians 3:28. "There is neither Jew nor Greek, there is neither slave nor free, there is neither male nor female; for you are all one in Christ Jesus." RSV

As I look through history, there are few, if any, women, who have left a mark in the world who always played by the rules. Most found ways to claim who they were and stand firmly in the presence of God, even when those in power thought they were wrong.

One of the things that often decreases our joy is denying who we are created to be. If you are created to dance, then dance. If you are created to be an incredible magnet for resources, then be that magnet. If you are called to teach, then teach. If you are…
I encourage you to think of Lydia the next time you hesitate, or even stop. Her hospitality was a real gift. Most likely her home became a place for the believers to meet. She had the resources. She had the desire. She was willing to step out. Are you?

Interpreting the Dream

As you think of your life so far, list some ways you have "stepped out" of your comfort zone to be fully present for God's dreams within and through you.

Has there been a time when you have not stepped out? If so, what was your reason?

Is there some way you are being called to step out right now? How do you know or sense this?

What would you need from God to have the courage to step out further?

Dream Walking

For today, as you are transitioning from one activity to the next, say, "I am called to step out by… (list three things without thinking)." Listen for God as you say these things and see if any of them are ones you are led to pursue. Do this multiple times throughout the day and open yourself to God's dreams for you.

Integrating the Dream

If possible, stand just before the threshold of a door. Stand straight and tall with your shoulders pulled back. Breathe in through your nose and out through your mouth. Put your hands together in front of you in the praying hands position. Lift your hands straight up and open them into a circle in front of you. See this circle as the dreams you and God are creating together. Step over the threshold and into these dreams. Bring your hands back into the praying hands position once again. Give thanks to God for dream walking with you. (For those unable to stand, this can be done using a wheelchair or visual imagery.)

Daily Prayer Journal

Date _____   Scripture _____

I rejoice in:
     1.
     2.
     3.
     4.
     5.

I hear God saying to me in the scripture:

Faith and visualization statements I am creating with God: (As you write today, review what you have been dreaming about with God. Does this alter what you desire to believe and visualize with God? Create a clear, concise, memorable statement that you can repeat prayerfully throughout the day.)

God and I dream about:

I commit to do the following things with God today:

Bridge from Whidby Island to Washington State
By Holly C. Rudolf

Day 23

"Set your heart on his kingdom and his goodness and all these things will come to you as a matter of course." Matthew 6:33 J.B. Phillips Translation

Reading for the Day: Matthew 6:25-34

Dreaming: Are You Searching for the Right Network?

What does your cell phone say when you turn it on? If I'm out of my home territory, mine says, "Searching for Network." I have found that it does no good for me to start dialing while the phone is searching. In fact, it actually slows the searching process down. It's as though I am confusing the phone by giving it too much information and too little time to hone in on its connection to the network of signals it needs to help me. The phone is of no use until it makes the initial connection with the network.

As I consider the many miracles in both the Old and the New Testaments, I am aware that at the beginning of each miracle there was someone who was seeking. There was someone who dared to dream that with God's help, the rules of the world need not apply. By seeking and connecting to God's dreams and ways first, the people got a small view of what could be. Because they saw what could be, they were willing to let go of what was and be open to a miracle.

Consider the friends of the man who cut a hole in a rooftop to lower him down to Jesus. The rules of this world would certainly say: "Wait your turn." "Don't damage property." "Be patient." "Miraculous healings don't happen." Yet they saw a different set of rules in God's kingdom. Rules like: "Each person matters." "Miraculous healings do happen." "God welcomes God's children who are most in need, even when that means others sometimes wait." They dared to dream their friend would be healed if they could get him to Jesus. They were right! All they sought was found, when they first sought God's desires for their friend. (Mark 2:1-12)

Or what about Elijah and the widow at Zarephath? Elijah was seeking to follow God and was hiding from Ahab. There was a famine throughout the land and he was starving. Elijah followed God's instructions and asked the widow woman for water and for food. She had planned to fix what little she had left for a final meal for herself and her son. She dared to see what the God of Elijah might actually do. Would Elijah's God keep the jug of oil flowing and the jar of meal filling until the rains would again come to the land? (1 Kings 17:8-16) God was, once again, more than faithful and provided in abundance.

Every miracle you will find in the Bible started with someone seeking and dreaming about what God could do with them and around them. God honored their search and desire with a miracle. I wonder how many times God has waited to do small and large things, simply because no one was open to dreaming and seeking and feeling the possibility that God's kingdom truly can come in moments today.

When you find things are not working, step back a moment and ask yourself, "Is what I'm doing really a part of God's ways?" If the answer is "no," then reconsider where and what you are seeking. If the answer is "yes," then continue to seek and trust and see where God and you are headed together. What can you dream with God's help? What miracles are you willing to accept and welcome?

Seeking and dreaming about God's ways and God's righteousness will guide us and help us to see that which we were formerly blind to in the limit of our own vision. Do we really want to be citizens of God's kingdom? If so, we must choose to connect with God's network of dreams first. When we discover we have short circuited our search for God's dreams with other interests, we need to purposefully redirect our minds and hearts.

It is a life long search, yet one worth making as we become more and more a part of the dreams and miracles God desires to share in us and through us.

Interpreting the Dream

If you were to live a day totally as a citizen of God's kingdom, what would you do with the day?

How is that vision the same as you spend a day now?

How is it different?

What does it mean or look like for you to seek God?

How will you do that today?

Dream Walking

For today, as you are transitioning from one activity to the next, say, "I am called to step out by… (list three things without thinking)." Listen for God as you say these things and see if any of them are ones you are led to pursue. Do this multiple times throughout the day and open yourself to God's dreams for you.

If you are musically inclined, look for the song, "Seek Ye First," by Karen Lafferty, copyright 1972, Maranatha! Music. Memorize it to sing to yourself and to God as a reminder of your opportunity to be a seeker. Or write a tune of your own to this verse, so you will be able to sing it readily to yourself as a reminder of your choice to seek God's dreams first.

Integrating the Dream

If possible, stand just before the threshold of a door. Stand straight and tall with your shoulders pulled back. Breathe in through your nose and out through your mouth. Put your hands together in front of you in the praying hands position. Lift your hands straight up and open them into a circle in front of you. See this circle as the dreams you and God are creating together. Step over the threshold and into these dreams. Bring your hands back into the praying hands position once again. Give thanks to God for dream walking with you. (For those unable to stand, this can be done using a wheelchair or visual imagery.)

Daily Prayer Journal

Date _____   Scripture _____

I rejoice in:
     1.
     2.
     3.
     4.
     5.

I hear God saying to me in the scripture:

Faith and visualization statements I am creating with God:

God and I dream about:

I commit to do the following things with God today:

Day 24

"Then they said to one another, 'What we are doing is wrong. This is a day of good news; if we are silent and wait until the morning light, we will be found guilty; therefore let us go and tell the king's household." 2 Kings 7:9 NRSV

Reading for the Day: 2 Kings 7:1-20

Dreaming: Are You Sure?

I used to think that menopause was one of those things talked about a lot, but rarely as intense or traumatic as the stories would suggest. I take it all back! The sweats, the waking up at night, the feeling like your heart will burst with the intensity of the heat rising up from within you and the intensification of emotions are all quite real. For many, they are a tough fought battle. I am amazed at the number of "solutions" that are out there. There are literally thousands of books, websites and "cures," all there to address a woman's needs and wants. I've tried several. There is very little I would not do if I could simply be assured the product would really work. Yet over time, I can, and have, become cynical. I listen to another's claims of great experiences and think, "Are you sure?" instead of "Hmm, maybe this is a solution."

There can come times in our lives when we, like the captain of the king in 2 Kings 7:2, hear what could be good news and are just unwilling to consider the possibility of hope in our situation. Now mind you, I can't even imagine what it must have been like in the city of Samaria. The people had been under siege by the Syrians and they were slowly starving. While the Syrians camped outside the town, feasting and laughing and waiting ever so patiently, the people of Samaria were dying. Some were even resorting to eating their children to survive. If the Samarians stayed in the city, they would die from lack of food. If they opened the gates, they knew they would certainly die by the swords of the Syrians or be taken as slaves. They had every reason to be terrified, frustrated and desperate. Is it any wonder that the captain questioned Elisha's sanity when he prophesied that precious food would sell cheaply the very next day?

Four lowly people, who had even less to lose than the captain, ventured out of their familiar spots at the entrance of the gate. These four lepers most likely knew nothing of Elisha's prophesy, but they were so tired of being stuck in a no-win situation, they were willing to try something different. They decided to walk into the Syrians' camp. If the Syrians had mercy, they would live. If they killed them, at least they would die quickly. The four ventured out at twilight. However, when they got to the edge of the Syrians' camp, no one was there. It was like a huge, empty, ghost camp. The lepers entered a tent and ate and drank to their hearts' content. How could this be? All their prayers for food, riches and safety had more than been answered. At this point, they did not know the Lord had made the Syrians hear the sounds of a mighty army so terrifying the Syrians had fled in the twilight, trying to save their own lives. All they knew was that they had been given an opportunity and, rather than question it or run from it, they dived right in. They even began to carry off silver, gold and clothing and hide it for their future use.

At one point, possibly because they feared the king or perhaps because they realized that good news was created to be shared, they returned to the city with the news of the Syrians' disappearance.

Not unlike me and perhaps you, the king questioned the good news. "Are you sure? Surely this is just a trap." It was one of the king's servants who finally convinced the king to send two men to check out the disappearance of the Syrians. What might have happened if the king had not been convinced it was worth the risk of checking out the good news? It was only after the messengers returned with an amazing report of the Syrians' complete departure that the people felt free to run out in joy and plunder the camp of the Syrians. Elisha's prophesy came true! Alas, the poor captain of the king did not live to see God's gift to the people. He was killed when the people ran over him at the gate on their way to the camp.

Sometimes life can feel a bit like a siege. When it seems that all the things we try do not result in success, we can begin to hold onto what we know, even if we are starving. We are afraid to try something new because it may be the wrong choice or perhaps someone would see us as foolish. The "Are you sure?" keeps sounding from our hearts and mouths, rather than expectancy that God will lead us out of the siege and into abundance.

I am not suggesting you try just anything, or do just anything. I am suggesting that with prayer, study and the company of others who are seeking God's ways, you need to be a bit adventurous and, yes, even hopeful. What if the lepers had not tried something different? Would the people have ever known that the source of their fear was gone? Would they have known that the answer to their hunger lay right outside the gates of the city?

Sieges will come in life. Things happen you will not be able to control. How will you meet them? How will you keep your heart open to God's dreams? Will you be persistent in dreaming and seeking God's guidance?

Interpreting the Dream

Think of a time in the past you have allowed yourself to feel under siege by life. Choose something you are not experiencing right now. Describe your feelings and thoughts.

What did you learn about yourself during the siege?

What did you learn about God during this time?

How did the end of this sense of being under siege come?

What skills, values or activities helped you to be open to God's leading during this time of feeling under siege?

Which of these are helpful tools to remember for the future?

If you are currently feeling under siege, what could you do differently that would create a new result?

Dream Walking

For today, as you are transitioning from one activity to the next, say, "I am called to step out by… (list three things without thinking)." Listen for God as you say these things and see if any of them are ones you are led to pursue. Do this multiple times throughout the day and open yourself to God's dreams for you.

Integrating the Dream

If possible, stand just before the threshold of a door. Stand straight and tall with your shoulders pulled back. Breathe in through your nose and out through your mouth. Put your hands together in front of you in the praying hands position. Lift your hands straight up and open them into a circle in front of you. See this circle as the dreams you and God are creating together. Step over the threshold and into these dreams. Bring your hands back into the praying hands position once again. Give thanks to God for dream walking with you. (For those unable to stand, this can be done using a wheelchair or visual imagery.)

Daily Prayer Journal

Date _____   Scripture _____

I rejoice in:
     1.
     2.
     3.
     4.
     5.

I hear God saying to me in the scripture:

Faith and visualization statements I am creating with God:

God and I dream about:

I commit to do the following things with God today:

Clowning Around
By Holly C. Rudolf

Day 25

"I assure you that the man who believes in me will do the same things that I have done, yes and he will do even greater things than these, for I am going away to the Father." John 14:12 J.B. Phillips Translation

Reading for the Day: John 14:12-18

Dreaming: Help Me to See God

Imagine a woman who listened for God each day. Her greatest desire was to hear God's voice and respond. One day in her prayers she heard she was to barbeque 8 chickens. She didn't know why, but trusted that just as she could already see and smell the chickens before she made them, God would show her who needed these chickens. Sure enough, when the chickens were done, people began to come to mind. There was a single mom who was struggling to feed her children, an older couple where the wife had recently come home from the hospital and was too weak to cook, a family with 6 children, etc. Each person who received a chicken had been praying for help. The woman's desire to trust God and act, even before she fully understood God's dream for the chickens, gave her the ability to touch many other lives. Great things were accomplished as she stepped up to be a true partner with God.

Whenever I read today's scripture passage, I am humbled. I am not out there healing the sick. I am not raising the dead. I am not looking into another's eyes and knowing all the sins and fears in their heart. What is it that Jesus was saying here? Who of us is really living up to this passage?

I am reminded anew of the haunting words of Gandhi, "If you Christians were more like your Christ, the whole world would be Christian." How right he was! Who would not want to follow one like Christ? What would it take to make me more like him, really more like him? Not the sweet and nicely packaged Christ, but the real resurrected Christ. What would it take for me to really do greater things than he did because he lives in me?

Christ had a dream. It was a dream inspired by his relationship with God. It was a dream that gave him the energy to stand and heal and feed more than 5000 people when he was weary. His dream allowed him to wander from place to place, never having the home most of us covet. His dream gave him the power to share a simple bread and cup with those he loved and with all of us centuries later, even when he knew he was about to be betrayed and crucified mercilessly. Jesus was not alone in these great acts. God was with him. And God, Jesus and the Holy Spirit are with me and with you.

I wonder sometimes how many opportunities I have let slide by me to partner with God in God's dreams. Maybe I thought I wasn't wise enough, or strong enough, or had enough time, or maybe I wasn't willing to pay the price the pursuit of the dream would cost me or those I love. How do you and I really perceive a part of God's dreams and choose to follow them?

For a long time, I thought prayer was about petitioning God, thanking God and praising God. These are all part of a healthy prayer life. However, one day as I was pondering the dream of writing this book and leading retreats and, yes, even being on

Oprah, it occurred to me it was not God that I needed to convince that these things could be a reality. It was me! God had known all along that the seed for this ministry was planted in me even before my birth. All God was trying to do was to help me see the seed and nurture it. All I needed to do was claim the mission, visualize it in its fullness and begin risking, investing and enjoying the process of creating this dream with God.

In part, prayer became me working and seeing God work through me, rather than expecting God to work and do it for me. Praise and thanksgiving naturally followed as I accepted my part in fulfilling this dream. It became clear to me that it was my responsibility to spend time each day visualizing the good this book would do in individual women's lives. I needed to see the woman who had given up on leading – lead; the woman who had given up on dancing – dance; the woman who had given up on dreaming – dream. I needed to trust that God had given, and was giving me, all I needed to be a part of the miracle of transformation in my life and in the lives of others.

God has called you to be a partner with God in something. The call from God won't always look the same. Sometimes the difference you make will be as dramatic as the feeding of the 5000. At other times, it will be as subtle as Jesus sitting down and talking with the children. Are you willing to let prayer plant the seed of God's dreams within you and transform you? Will you be available as God's daughters to run, work, laugh, sweat, grow and live out God's dreams within you? This is my prayer.

Interpreting the Dream

Without screening your ideas, list ideas or dreams you have had since you were a child. What are the dreams you always wished you would have followed up on, but for whatever reason decided it was forever to be "only a dream."

Look over your list. Of all these items, which one or two do you feel would glorify God and use more of your talents? Are you committed to praying for and visualizing the completion of this idea or dream, even if you work with God on it for many years? If so, write one sentence that describes your dream and commit to repeating this statement a minimum of 10 times a day until the dream comes to fruition. If you are musically inclined, set it to a tune. Include a date by when you desire to accomplish it. List what you are willing to do to make this dream a reality. I look forward to you sharing with me the dreams you are led to pursue. Email me at dreamwalkingdrh@yahoo.com and put Dream Walking in the subject line. I will be happy to lift you up in prayer when I receive your email.

My dream of faith is:

I will accomplish this with God's help by _____ (date).

I will commit to the following activities to make this dream come true:

As you repeat this statement, be sure to visualize yourself in the midst of the fullness of living out the dream. Give thanks for the visions and dreams God chooses to share with you, God's valued partner in ministry.

Dream Walking

Talk to a woman who is over 70 years old. What dreams did she have as a young person? Which ones did she pursue? Which ones did she not pursue? What helped her to decide to pursue or give up? Did anything she dreamed about seem impossible, yet it became a reality many times greater than the dream as life unfolded? What does she dream about today?

For today, as you are transitioning from one activity to the next, say, "I am called to step out by… (list three things without thinking)." Listen for God as you say these things and see if any of them are ones you are led to pursue. Do this multiple times throughout the day and open yourself to God's dreams for you.

Integrating the Dream

If possible, stand just before the threshold of a door. Stand straight and tall with your shoulders pulled back. Breathe in through your nose and out through your mouth. Put your hands together in front of you in the praying hands position. Lift your hands straight up and open them into a circle in front of you. See this circle as the dreams you and God are creating together. Step over the threshold and into these dreams. Bring your hands back into the praying hands position once again. Give thanks to God for dream walking with you. (For those unable to stand, this can be done using a wheelchair or visual imagery.)

Daily Prayer Journal

Date _____   Scripture _____

I rejoice in:

     1.

     2.

     3.

     4.

     5.

I hear God saying to me in the scripture:

Faith and visualization statements I am creating with God:

God and I dream about:

I commit to do the following things with God today:

Day 26

"Make me to know your ways, O LORD; teach me your paths." Psalm 25:4   NRSV

Reading for the Day: Psalm 25

Dreaming: Open My Ears

I woke up this morning, Lord, and I knew I needed to talk with Julie Hefley about her life and singing ministry. There was no burning bush or loud voice, just a strong, quiet inner voice telling me this was important to both Julie's ministry and mine.

Just the night before, we sat close to each other working on paperwork and watching our children practice for a dance in a musical. I hadn't felt led to talk to her then. Now, as I walked into the theatre to watch practice once again, I scanned the room hoping to see her. There she was, sitting alone and far enough back we could talk and not disturb the practice. We did the usual chit chat and I began to look for some way to say, "By the way, God told me to talk with you today." (Oddly enough not everyone just jumps at the opportunity when you put it that way.)

With a little effort, our conversation was launched – everything from how her CD could work with retreats I lead to a recording studio that could help Bill with his music to encouraging one another to step out in faith. Somewhere in the conversation, I shared with her my sense that God had led me to talk to her. She smiled and nodded knowingly. She shared a few stories of times when God had guided her to specific people and places to help clarify and expand her ministry.

It has been a difficult thing as an adult to listen for and trust God's voice within me. I went through a period in my faith life as an adolescent when I was very emotional. Many would even say I was fanatical about my faith. I grew very close to God through this period, so close that I began to hear and acknowledge my call to be a minister. I was very excited and shared my calling with some of the adult leaders of our group. In their minds, my call to ministry was not from God at all. They recommended I find a young man who wanted to be a pastor and marry him, becoming his helpmate. If that didn't work, it would be fine for me to teach children and other women, but I should never be a pastor in a church. They shared scriptures with me and I listened intently to these people of faith, who had in many ways taught me a great deal about God. How was I to reconcile their view with the ever-growing call to ministry I felt? Their understanding left no room for me if I pursued my calling to ministry. The dissonance within me grew as the dream of ministry I had growing within me became more and more distinct from the ideas of those who were teaching me.

About this time, I had an incredible dream. More than thirty years later, I can remember it in detail. I was lying on my back and a very large book opened above me. I could see nothing but its pages. I began to read and recognized scripture after scripture. I was in awe. The page turned and I heard a voice read to me the words I saw printed in large bold letters, "He who teaches my children falsely will die." The book suddenly slammed shut and I sat up in bed with my heart beating rapidly. What had just happened? Who was teaching falsely? How was I to respond? I prayed late into the night. I knew I did not have all the answers. However, I vowed I would be very careful what I believed and taught others.

The dream set in motion a lifelong journey for me. I determined I would study the scriptures for myself and discern who God is without being told by others who may or may not be right. I would encourage others to read, study and pursue God. At that time, my associate minister, Dick Hamm, guided me to a book, Your God Is Too Small by J.B. Phillips. I read the book eagerly and completed an independent study of J.B. Phillips' works with Susan Young, an amazing public high school English teacher, who shared her faith with me and encouraged me to pursue God and my calling to ministry fully.

While my new pursuit of personal knowledge of God, Jesus and the Holy Spirit, was a gift and a blessing, I somehow started to classify the hearing of God's voice through the Holy Spirit, with people in the "fanatical" groups. It was as though I had on headsets that played only certain types of music. I did not know what I did not know, because I could not hear it directly. Yet God certainly did not stop speaking and guiding me in God's ways. Even then, God would find ways of leading me through scripture and experiences, yet I was just not able to hear God's voice within me because it was not something I was expecting or seeking.

When my children were small, they ever so clearly and innocently would talk with me about God talking with them. There was no surprise or shame in this for them. It was beautiful, expected and accepted. I grew to hunger for the simplicity they experienced talking with God. In moments when I became more willing to listen without my chosen headsets, I, too, would hear God's voice. At points I was even able to respond. I seek that voice now. I certainly do not and cannot control when it comes, but I am so thankful when I hear God's voice clearly. What a joy it is when I pursue that voice and find that I am either able to be the answer to someone else's prayer or they are the answer to mine.

Someone once asked me how I knew the voice was God's. I don't always. I listen and see if what the voice is saying fits with the ways of God I have learned. Does pursuing the guidance of the voice bring greater love, hope, joy, mercy, justice or forgiveness into the world? Does responding to the voice seem to take me in the direction of growing into the woman God is calling me to be? Do I sense the Holy Spirit is present in the voice? If I'm not sure, sometimes I ask for clarification or I wait. This certainly worked for Gideon (Judges 6:36-40) and Samuel (1 Samuel 3), as well as others.

I encourage you to seek to hear the voice of God. Hunger after the Holy Spirit. Be open to its quiet, and sometimes not so quiet, urgings. How deep of a friendship would you have with your beloved if you never spoke with and listened to one another? We know for certain that when Christ needed guidance he prayed and he listened. (Matthew 26:36-46) He taught us to pray freely to God. Open our ears, God, that we might hear and respond to Your dreams for all of humanity.

Interpreting the Dream

If you have not already begun to use the daily prayer exercise, be sure to use it today. Review how you have been using it if you started it at the beginning of this series. After time in the scripture and prayer, you are asked to list a few things God wants to do with you today. Sometimes it helps to just begin writing. Don't worry about whether you have the resources or the time. When you have completed the list, review it with God and listen to God's voice within you. Which of these are important to fulfilling God's dreams within you?

Be sure to review this list each day. If anything is unfinished, decide with God if it should be moved into another day until completed or if it is no longer relevant. Use this format to help you to focus more clearly on God's presence and partnership with you in each day.

Dream Walking

What do you remember learning or hearing about God speaking to people? What did your family of origin believe? What are the stories that come to mind?

How does God speak to you?

Is this the same or different than how you experienced God speaking to you 10 years ago?

Take time today to be quiet for a few minutes at least twice. Ask God to speak to you of things that are important to God and then listen. What is God currently doing that you can be a part of right now? Just as a parent is honored by a child seeking their council and partnering with them, so is God honored and pleased when we seek to partner with God in God's work.

For today, as you are transitioning from one activity to the next, say, "I am called to step out by... (list three things without thinking)." Listen for God as you say these things and see if any of them are ones you are led to pursue. Do this multiple times throughout the day and open yourself to God's dreams for you.

Integrating the Dream

If possible, stand just before the threshold of a door. Stand straight and tall with your shoulders pulled back. Breathe in through your nose and out through your mouth. Put your hands together in front of you in the praying hands position. Lift your hands straight up and open them into a circle in front of you. See this circle as the dreams you and God are creating together. Step over the threshold and into these dreams. Bring your hands back into the praying hands position once again. Give thanks to God for dream walking with you. (For those unable to stand, this can be done using a wheelchair or visual imagery.)

Daily Prayer Journal

Date _____   Scripture _____

I rejoice in:

     1.

     2.

     3.

     4.

     5.

I hear God saying to me in the scripture:

Faith and visualization statements I am creating with God:

God and I dream about:

I commit to do the following things with God today:

Two Girls Ready and Waiting
By Thomas Russell

Day 27

"That is why I say to you, Don't worry about living—wondering what you are going to eat or drink, or what you are going to wear. Surely life is more important than food and the body more important than the clothes you wear. Look at the birds in the sky. They never sow nor reap nor store away in barns and yet your Heavenly Father feeds them. Aren't you much more valuable to him than they are?" Matthew 6:25-26   J.B. Phillips Translation

Reading for the Day: Matthew 6:25-34

Dreaming: Dare to Dream

I read this passage this morning and it challenged me to a whole new way of thinking. Funny how passages that are old and familiar can speak to us in fresh ways, opening up a part of life that before was an unknown door. I've always seen this passage from the perspective of not getting concerned about material things.

However, today what I heard Jesus telling me was, "Don't worry." What is it about worry that goes beyond raising the blood pressure, stressing the heart and creating an irritating person to be around that is not good for us and for the fulfillment of God's dreams in us? A critical key is in Matthew 7:7-8. "Ask, and it will be given to you; search, and you will find; knock, and the door will be opened for you. For everyone who asks receives, and everyone who searches finds, and for everyone who knocks, the door will be opened." NRSV What if this scripture is more a statement of fact in the way God has created the universe and our part in it to be, instead of something God actively does to us or for us? What if that which we ask, that which we attend to, that which we give our energy and creativity to, naturally comes to us – in a sense we attract it? When we worry, we actually attract to ourselves that which we are worrying about. When we trust that God will provide for our material needs, this too happens, because what we are attracting is the completion of our trusting.

This concept makes me a bit nervous because it requires me to really take responsibility for my casual thoughts and words. What am I speaking into being when I worry? What could I be partnering with God to create if I choose to focus my thinking and feeling and believing towards something else? If we as Christians begin to worry less about the state of the world and dream more about fulfilling the dreams of God for all of God's people, what could be accomplished?

I think of Dr. Martin Luther King, Jr. Surely he must have had days when he was too weary to dream. Yet he understood that worrying about those who hated him, focusing only on his anger about the injustices that existed and surrendering to his fears, would create only more of the same. He chose to "have a dream."

Without overshadowing the painful realities of segregation in the present, he chose to dream in amazing ways about what could be and should be if God's dreams were lived out by God's people. Over and over again in his speech, "I Have a Dream," given on August 28, 1963, Dr. King provided images of life lived with hope and fullness without segregation and prejudice.

I encourage you to read this speech in its entirety as a part of your prayer today. It can be found on several websites or at your library. The power of the full speech is one that has brought hope and the desire to dream anew to thousands of weary souls.

As I hear Dr. King's words anew, it causes me to wonder what might happen if you and I freed ourselves to dream with God again. Could there be a world without AIDS, instead of so many of us worrying about people we love getting this awful disease? Could there be peace instead of violence in our homes and in our world? What if you and I dreamed of a world where children are cherished and loved wherever they live instead of worrying over the rise of abuse? For when you and I really dream of something, we become an active part of the realization of that dream. We begin to act, feel, trust and work as though it is true. We make the dream real first in ourselves and then we help to create it in others.

Today, God, the word I hear is to "stop worrying." I hear You crying out to all of us to trust You and believe that Your dreams can dwell within us. I hear You pleading with us to dream Your dreams and to strive to fulfill them with You. I hear Your desire for us to be real partners with You in creating your reality of love, truth, justice, grace, creativity and power.

Give us the strength and wisdom to fervently ask, seek and knock for the desires of Your heart, that we might help to attract and create them. God, help us today to spend our energy believing that we might be a part of creating new realities with You. May we sacrifice our worry today that we might step more fully into Your dreams for us and for Your world.

Interpreting the Dream

If you are prone to worrying or complaining, think for a moment of the top one or two things that seem to be repeating issues for you. Write these down. Sit quietly in prayer and with God imagine what the opposite of your worry or complaint is. When you have a clear picture in your mind, write or draw this. Stop and repeat aloud the words you have written or describe the picture. Claim this as a reality in your life. For example, if you are concerned about how well you are parenting a child, list words that describe characteristics of a strong parent to you. See yourself parenting well. See your child responding and thriving. Feel the gift of seeing you and your child relating in ways that bring life and hope to both of you. When you find yourself worrying over these issues again, remind yourself of the way you and God desire things to be. What dream do you have? Hold fast to this dream and cleanse your mind from worry or complaints.

Dream Walking

For today, as you are transitioning from one activity to the next, say, "I am called to step out by… (list three things without thinking)." Listen for God as you say these things and see if any of them are ones you are led to pursue. Do this multiple times throughout the day and open yourself to God's dreams for you.

Integrating the Dream

If possible, stand just before the threshold of a door. Stand straight and tall with your shoulders pulled back. Breathe in through your nose and out through your mouth. Put your hands together in front of you in the praying hands position. Lift your hands straight up and open them into a circle in front of you. See this circle as the dreams you and God are creating together. Step over the threshold and into these dreams. Bring your hands back into the praying hands position once again. Give thanks to God for dream walking with you. (For those unable to stand, this can be done using a wheelchair or visual imagery.)

Daily Prayer Journal

Date _____   Scripture _____

I rejoice in:
      1.
      2.
      3.
      4.
      5.

I hear God saying to me in the scripture:

Faith and visualization statements I am creating with God:

God and I dream about:

I commit to do the following things with God today:

Shakertown, Kentucky – Interpreter Dancing "Tis a Gift to Be Simple
By Holly C. Rudolf

Day 28

"More to be desired are they than gold, even much fine gold, sweeter also than honey and drippings of the honeycomb." Psalm 19:10   RSV

Reading for the Day: Psalm 19:1-14

Dreaming: Savoring the Word

Do you remember your first love? The one that made your heart sing, had you waiting at the phone or running to be twirled in laughter? Maybe that love was well placed and lasting or maybe it was temporary. However, I am guessing you can remember how it felt.

In Psalm 19 the writer speaks of God's Word with this same type of passion and desire. In beautiful poetic language he creates the image of God's Word being more valuable than gold or the sweetest honey. These Words alone can revive the soul, make wise the simple, bring rejoicing, enlighten the eyes and endure forever. It is God's Words, made clear by Jesus and the Holy Spirit, that open us to see who God is and who God is calling us to be. It is God's Words that challenge us to leave behind our sleep walking and open ourselves to dream walking with God again.

I am amazed that God continues to speak with us. Just as with Adam and Eve, Peter, Lydia, Paul and others, God stays in relationship with us even when we are distant and distracted by our lack of awareness. God's Words continue to be everywhere — in scripture, in God's creation, in our dreams, on the lips of others and in that inner voice that is sometimes still and quiet and at other times very loud. As we immerse ourselves in God's Words they wash over us and bring newness of life. We savor them and find new tastes and nourishment. God's Word is truly something to be cherished and embraced throughout the seasons of life.

I pray that in these 28 days you have heard more and more of God's Words for you as you have made the time to study, pray and dream with God. As a woman, you have unique powers and gifts to bring to the world, a world that is hungry to dream again. May you dream of a world where God's Words are made real for every person. May you dream of a world where every man, woman and child knows that God loves them, not just in their heads, but in their hearts as well. May you see a world where every person knows that God smiles when God's children of all ages work in unity to make God's wonderful dreams come true. May you dream of a world in which the daily activity of humanity brings more smiles than tears to the face of God.

I invite you to dream with me and to believe that God does do great things in us and through us. Savor these Words of promise. Drink these Words of promise. Live these Words of promise. I will look forward each day to hearing and seeing the dreams of God rise up from you, my sisters in faith. Feel free to contact me at dreamwalkingdrh@yahoo.com to share the experiences you have dreaming with God. It is in living and sharing our dreams, that we begin to create networks of dreamers and inspire one another to pursue the dreams God has for us individually and as a people.

May the One who created you to dream and love be particularly close to you today and always. Let it be so.

"Let the words of my mouth and the meditation of my heart be acceptable in Thy sight, O Lord, my rock and my redeemer." (Psalm 19:14) NAS

Interpreting the Dream

What are some of the Words of God that come to mind today that you are savoring?

On Day 2 you were asked to complete the following scale. Without looking at your previous answers, please respond to the following:

On a scale of 1 -10, 1 being not at all and 10 being always, rate with an "X" how much of your God-given identity and joy is visible in what you do in the following areas of your life:

Marriage or significant relationships

1	2	3	4	5	6	7	8	9	10

Church life/spiritual life

1	2	3	4	5	6	7	8	9	10

Work life

1	2	3	4	5	6	7	8	9	10

Family Life

1	2	3	4	5	6	7	8	9	10

Recreational time

1	2	3	4	5	6	7	8	9	10

Life Maintenance Duties

1	2	3	4	5	6	7	8	9	10

Go back through and with an "O" mark how often you dream with God about creating new possibilities in these areas. When completed, notice the difference or the similarities in your markings from Day 2 to Day 28. What comes to mind as you view these scales?

What gleanings and prayer disciplines do you desire to carry into your next 28 days of dream walking with God?

Dream Walking

If you are completing this study on your own, find a cup of tea and three or four sweet spices you enjoy smelling and tasting. Brew the tea and add each ingredient as you consider some of the gifts God has given you in your dream walking together. How do the spices blend together? How have your dreams blended into your daily living? Drink the tea slowly and savor these gifts as you imagine them flowing into your body, warming and supporting you as you taste, smell and feel the tea.

If you have been doing this study with a group, make a celebration of the conclusion. Each woman may bring two or three sweet spices for tea. Create a banquet table and share the spices. Enjoy this time together and speak of the gifts you have received from God and from one another as you savor the tea. Be sure to have some honey on your table as well.

Listen to the song, "Well Done," by Bill Rose-Heim. The song may be downloaded from www.nwareacc.org . Imagine God singing this song to you.

Integrating the Dream

If possible, stand just before the threshold of a door. Stand straight and tall with your shoulders pulled back. Breathe in through your nose and out through your mouth. Put your hands together in front of you in the praying hands position. Lift your hands straight up and open them into a circle in front of you. See this circle as the dreams you and God are creating together. Step over the threshold and into these dreams. Bring your hands back into the praying hands position once again. Give thanks to God for dream walking with you. (For those unable to stand, this can be done using a wheelchair or visual imagery.)

Daily Prayer Journal

Date _____   Scripture _____

I rejoice in:
     1.
     2.
     3.
     4.
     5.

I hear God saying to me in the scripture:

Faith and visualization statements I am creating with God:

God and I dream about:

I commit to do the following things with God today:

Appendix A: Visualization Technique

Visualization is a method of prayer that helps us to see things as they could be. In visualizing we maintain awareness and can start or stop at any time. I have been asked during retreats if visualization is "safe." The person was concerned that visualization could be an opportunity for evil to control them. I told them I believed God has given us the gift to visualize. Like any other gift, we choose to use it for good or for evil. By focusing our visualizations on growing in God, I believe we have a powerful tool to help us grow exponentially and be more aware of opportunities God desires to share with us. As we separate ourselves from the many external distractions, we can focus more intently on God and our souls. In a sense, we take a mini-retreat with God. If at any point someone feels visualization is taking them in a direction she does not feel is led by God, she can immediately stop.

Like other types of activities, it is helpful to have a method by which you start visualization. Just like driving a car, the steps will at first seem unfamiliar and then will become a natural response each time you wish to pray through visualization. Though there are many different methods, the following is a process that I have found to be fruitful.

Find a comfortable chair or sitting position on the floor. For each person this is different. Some may prefer to lie down, however sleep can frequently happen in a fully relaxed state. Ask God to bless this time of prayerful visualization. Breathe in through your nose and out through your mouth slowly three times. Think of yourself breathing in God's spirit and breathing out all that which is not bringing you closer to God.

Focus on your feet. Tighten your feet for three seconds and then relax them. Experience the feeling of letting go and relaxing. Imagine God's spirit flowing into you through the top of your head and into your feet. Tighten your legs for three seconds and relax them. Notice again God's Spirit flowing into you. Tighten your abdomen for three seconds and relax it. Tighten your chest for three seconds and relax it. Remember to continue to breathe deeply. Use the same method to relax your arms and hands. Focus on your head. Intentionally relax your face and jaw. Imagine God's Spirit flowing in through the top of your head. Think of yourself as a vessel that is being filled with God's Spirit from your toes to the top of your head.

When you are fully relaxed breathe in and out three times again. Imagine yourself in a setting where you feel safe and joyful. This could be a real place or a combination of real and imagined settings. Enjoy this place. What do you hear, see, feel and experience? Spend some time here enjoying this place. You see a trail and begin to walk on it. What does the trail look and feel like? You see an opening up ahead and there you see a church, a house, a cave or even a womb. This is a place you can go whenever you want to really focus on your relationship with God. Enter this place and make yourself comfortable.

From this sanctuary, you can visualize speaking with God, imagine options, invent something, study scripture, etc. By allowing yourself to be focused in this place new options can rise up through you taking time to dream with God. Be aware of what you see, hear and feel. Experience fully this place for creating and dreaming with God.

When you are ready to stop visualizing, give thanks to God for your experience. Ask God to help you apply that which is dream fulfilling. Share any words or feelings that are important to you. Imagine you are leaving your inner sanctuary. Head back down the trail to your original visualized setting. This, too, is a place you may choose to dream with God.

At any point during visualization you are free to open your eyes. Give yourself time to adjust to the world around you. Breathe in and out three times. Breathe in through your nose and out through your mouth. Consider the gleanings of the visualization.

As you increase your practice of visualization, it will become easier for you to enter more quickly into a relaxed state. Take the time in the beginning to fully relax your body. This enhances your ability to visualize as you are less attentive to your physical comfort.

Appendix B

Daily Prayer Journal

Date _____   Scripture _____

I rejoice in:
1.
2.
3.
4.
5.

I hear God saying to me in the scripture:

Faith and visualization statements I am creating with God:

God and I dream about:

I commit to do the following things with God today:

Those wishing to purchase **Dream Walking** for groups or gifts, may purchase 5 or more copies for $8 a book from the author. Shipping fees are $4.50 for one book and $10 for 3 - 6 books. Orders may be placed through www.DreamWalkingWithGod.com, by email at dreamwalkingdrh@yahoo.com , or mailed to 705 East Third, Cameron, MO 64429.

❧ Dream Support Section ❧

You are encouraged to email your experiences of dreaming with God to dreamwalkingdrh@yahoo.com. Please put "Dream Walking" in the subject line. As we celebrate the many things God does with us through our dreaming, we create a powerful network of women dreaming around the world and choosing to act on those dreams. Your stories may be shared in presentations, retreats and interviews, as well as potentially be included in a future book.

Discussion groups using **Dream Walking** for study, are welcome to schedule a 20 minute phone call with Donna. Visit her website at www.DreamWalkingWithGod.com or contact her by email at dreamwalkingdrh@yahoo.com to schedule your group.